The

Indian

Water

Slide

With Best wishes

Phil Schuster

A novel by
Philip F. Schuster

The characters and events in this book are fictitious.
Place names as well as the names of Indian family and
clan names are real. Any other similarity to real persons,
living or dead, is coincidental and not intended by the author.

ISBN 0-9670932-0-1

Library of Congress Catalog Card Number: 99-71097

On the cover: Opal Creek Wilderness, Oregon
by Larry N. Olson, photographer
Copyright © 1999 Larry N. Olson

Printed in the United States of America by
Maverick Publications, Inc. • Bend, Oregon

ACKNOWLEDGEMENTS

I am most grateful to my colleague, friend and mentor, Roger F. Dierking, for his encouragement and inspiration during our many long walks — partnership meetings — along the Columbia River. Mr. Dierking's deep commitment to family and environmental issues, as well as his insight and intellect, have been invaluable resources in the writing of this book. Many of the ideas for this book stem from cases Mr. Dierking and I have undertaken over the past two decades.

There is one friend of mine whose modesty would not permit him to be mentioned. Without his countless hours of editing and without the benefit of his excellent ideas and superb writing skills, this book would not have become a reality. You know who you are and I thank you from the bottom of my heart.

I am also especially grateful to Barbara Olsen and to Heather Munday for the many long hours they spent typing and proofreading. In addition, I am very indebted to the fine staff at Maverick Publications.

I wish to thank writer Timothy R. Brown for his thoughtful help in reading and critiquing the manuscript. I also thank Morris E. Belgard, member of the White Clay Society, Gros Ventre Tribe of the Fort Belknap Indian Reservation, for his fine suggestions.

My heartfelt thanks goes to my mother and to other family members and friends, including those who are no longer with us — most notably my late father, Philip F. Schuster.

Above all, I am indebted beyond measure to my wife, Barbara, and to my children, Chris and Matt, without whose presence, encouragement and love I would not have been able to write this book.

For Barbara, Chris and Matt

CONTENTS

CHAPTER 1

THE ROGUE

The letter from the state of Oregon was waiting for him at home. Another summons for him to appear in court. Ron's gut ached as he pictured himself confronted by a black-robed judge, his hostile eyes boring down, right through him.

To the lone black crow circling high above, Ron Hathaway's beaten Ford pickup must have seemed insignificant, crawling northward on Interstate 5 as the freeway slowly unrolled along the thick green carpet of the Willamette Valley.

It had been a hard, ten-hour day at the construction site in Drain, about an hour's drive southeast of his home in Springfield. Thoughts of his first Rogue whitewater trip with Melissa made the drab, gray day seem pleasant. Ron had kept at this job in Drain for Dahlberg Construction Company longer than any of his others. Ron's tall, lanky forty-five year old frame was tired and dirty — he was self-conscious about his black fingernails — oil from the engine of a construction rig.

Ron Hathaway mulled over the letter again. As he did so, he recalled his most recent telephone conversation with Melissa earlier in the day. He always called her from the small diner off the road about a mile due west — down a forest-corridored road — from the job site in Drain. She would wait for his call which came promptly at 12:45 in the afternoon.

"Hi hon," Ron had said enthusiastically.

"Hi, handsome. Like the lunch?" Melissa would make his lunches and always slip a note in — on a napkin or a small piece of paper. This time, she wrote about what they'd do when they were alone together after their Friday night out with friends.

"I ate your note," he whispered back at her with a mischievous chuckle.

"You keep your cap on today?" she teased again. Melissa loved the way his Caterpillar hat pushed his already protruding ears out even further.

Ron grinned to himself.

"Did ya get ahold of Sharon to see if Karin can babysit for us tonight?" he asked, anxious that there be no foul-ups for this evening.

"She promised me that she would remind that daughter of hers she has to babysit tonight," said Melissa. Karin Gunderson, their neighbor's fifteen-year-old daughter, loved to babysit. Like most teenagers, though, she had an agenda as busy as the President's.

"Get any mail? Did the letter from your folks come?" Ron asked, to change the subject.

"Yeah, got their letter and a bunch of bills to boot."

"Same old, same old, I guess," Ron said.

"Well, you did get a letter addressed to you from the state of Oregon," replied Melissa. Ron winced.

"Go ahead and see what those gumshoes want," he said. "I'm sick and tired of their pestering me, dammit." Ron Hathaway's head started to throb.

"Are you sure you want me to open the letter?"

"Ah, I don't care, honey — don't worry about it," he told her, not particularly wanting to let his wife know how upset he was and suddenly wanting to change the subject again. "Let's not talk about it tonight, O.K., hon?"

"O.K.," she promised. They turned their attention to their Friday night activities and to plans he had for installing a hot tub behind their house. He spoke to her of his dreams and she teased him some more. They laughed and made plans for the coming summer — to drift, perhaps, the John Day River or the Rogue again. Then Ron Hathaway told Melissa when he would be home and told her to pick "a candle to light for us tonight." This was another of his special signals to her.

Melissa's parting tease left Ron with a warm feeling. His attention became fixed to the semicircular streaks and stains on his windshield. The wipers rhythmically swept the rain, creating a kind of hypnotic effect. Ron's thoughts drifted.

* * * * *

The brown bear in camp that evening had frightened Ron Hathaway to death, although he had never admitted this to his wife. The immense, hairy creature, finished with pounding the blue and white cooler to pieces, sauntered toward their tent perched on a Rogue

River sand embankment, close-in to the scrub trees and fir. Melissa, sitting bolt upright from the sleeping bag, peered out of the flap. Ron, panic stricken, thought of how he would cut his way out of the back side of the tent.

"'Lissa, for chrissakes, give me the goddamned knife!" Ron implored. He had always taken his father's huge, ivory-handled hunting knife on drift trips — he kept it in the cooler. He remembered this painful fact now, as he watched his young wife's reaction at the front of the tent.

"Shush," she whispered. "Don't move. Don't even breathe." Ron was awestruck at her apparent coolness.

"Shit, he's gonna eat us alive!" Ron blurted out, his heart bursting with adrenaline.

"Knock it off!" she blew back in a hoarse whisper. Ron's eyes were riveted to the back of her head. She was poised, on her toes now, hands slightly raised. Melissa had always been fearless.

Ron grew even more horrified as he watched the bear continue lumbering towards the front tent flap, not more than a hundred feet away. His Colt .45 automatic offered no protection now, tucked away at home. The animal came on like some huge hunchbacked creature carrying a dark shawl, swaying from side to side. Looking directly at the thing, Ron never forgot the eyes glinting at him from the reflected moonlight. He felt the terror strike him once again. Beady, steely, cold — fathomless — inert.

Suddenly the bear's attention seemed captivated by a mystery off to the side. The bear turned and ambled off down the sand embankment, over the rocks and around the boulders beside the river.

Ron felt the wet drizzle gently touch his left arm, cocked out of the open window of his old truck. His grin was the only outward sign of the memory he held of that Rogue River excursion with Melissa.

It was the first July of their marriage. The emerald and white Rogue River murmured and glimmered as it gently glided — on that first morning out — past the town of Galice, a little cranny pieced together with a few cedar shake stores, a gas station and a blazing tin-roofed restaurant perched by the river.

The hills, strewn with wildflowers, and covered with groves of hemlock, myrtlewood and Douglas fir, formed a rich, living tapestry, as the Rogue River Valley folded itself around the glinting Rogue River, splintering the sunlight into sparkling rivulets. Huge boulders, dead trees, branches and brush-lined back eddies — a colossal rock garden — sculpted the character of this green primordial place.

He remembered that it was a Saturday during this July Rogue journey with Melissa when he'd finally edged his inflatable boat — nicknamed the "Tiger Tub" — over a low sandbank in a little shaded back eddy.

At Paradise Lodge Ron and Melissa stopped and sipped coffee together out on the stone veranda on the bluff above the river. Later they discovered the small grassy airfield out back next to the side of the forested hill facing the river. They leisurely walked among the trees and cedar cabins next to the lodge. They stood on top of the bluff and talked of their plans. That's when Ron told her about the special place on Tate Creek.

Ron saw the buck standing off to the right of the boat, its legs hidden in the tall grass covering the small jetty. Sensing his boat, the deer jerked its antlers upwards, as if beckoning to him, and bounded off into the thick underbrush. This time, he and Melissa, holding the wet and crumpled river map, tromped over the raised sandy alcove. They entered the thick reedy grass and scrub brush and moved slowly into the moss-covered trees. They hiked about 200 yards up along a shadowy, dirt incline which followed the creek inland, snaking under broken fir branches, over mossy boulders and around huge rotting trunks. Melissa would never forget where Ron took her that day, of the sight she saw below them on the path when they finally reached their Tate Creek destination.

A quiet, shadowy pool reflected the over-arching firs. It lay directly underneath the sloping rock cliff setback. A circular clearing below them surrounded the pebbled edges of the pool. A stream of water slid down and off of the semicircular hollow of the rock, eons of time having shaped the smooth, gray rock cliff into a shiny, hollowed out slide. They stared in awe. The slide, set at an incline of about forty-five degrees, was a funnel-like chute which had been embedded in the folds of the rock cliff by the natural architects, wind and water, of this sacred place. How many Takelma, Shasta Costa or Chetco Indian children had frolicked over the centuries here? The top was nestled amid the standing forest, sunlight casting bent tree shadows across the curved surface of the hollowed out rock. Water gently rolled and weaved down through the chute and then bubbled out below like a gargoyle spigot. The soft splashing reverberated off the rock walls, as the water cascaded six feet down into the deep end of the dark pool below.

Ron waded through the shallows of the pool next to the cliff and took hold of a slippery rope. It was old and frayed and secured to the cliff in a manner perhaps only the local gods understood. Ron climbed up ahead of Melissa, while she stood below and watched. He inched up, terrified the rope would break, eyes glued to the slippery rock in front of him. Near the top, his breathing became labored. The sockets of his eyes hurt. His knees wobbled, his legs shook, especially his war-injured left leg. Ron glanced around, hoping to find a level landing spot, realizing only at this point that the ladder ended and he must now crawl on his stomach over the rounded top of the tall boulder without help. He saw nothing he could grasp except slippery rock. He looked down, hoping to get a glimmer of reassurance from Melissa. The cliff and trees started to swirl. He closed his eyes. He felt unsteady. His breathing stopped. Still he couldn't let himself falter in front of Melissa.

In a panic-stricken frenzy, he scrambled to the top. Then he paused to feel the cool water trickling through his fingers. He now opened his eyes completely. In an instant, Melissa was seated next to him, her arm around his shoulder. He felt weak. He couldn't move his legs.

"This is really fun!" Melissa exclaimed.

Christ, Ron thought, even if the bear didn't get me, this chute sure as shit will. Ron was quivering. Got to stop this, he insisted to himself. He summoned all his courage which proved to be just enough to carry him through.

"I'll go first," he shivered with a crooked smile.

Melissa laughed.

Now, in his truck, Ron remembered the mingled fear and exhilaration as he sat exhausted and trembling on top of the tall boulder. He finally went first, Melissa coaxing him, he sitting in the cup of the rock, letting the cool water build up behind his naked back. Melissa gently nudged him with her toe. He slid down. For an instant Ron closed his eyes and felt as if he was taking the first drop on a roller coaster ride. Then the cool water enveloped him. He felt calm, serene. Reaching the surface he turned and saw Melissa, sliding down to meet him. Then her beautiful, milky smooth legs stretched out and met his, in that secret place, in the quietness of the pool.

Dusty bands of sunlight pierced the dancing shadows of the fir trees that afternoon, wrapping warmth around their merging bodies. The ancient time of the gods and Indian children came back to them through the gentle swaying of the reflecting pool. Their nakedness became as much a natural part of each other as the water, spouting from the slide, and became forever merged with their memories of the mystic and quiet pool.

Ron held Melissa more tenderly than any other woman he had known before. He felt the softness of her skin, her heartbeat pulsating against his chest. He smelled the pungent sap and musky bark and moss odor of the forest, mixed with the sweetness of her auburn hair and her warm, moist body. He beheld her eyes and heard the soft murmurings from her lips, her sweet breath against his ear, the water echoing back as it trickled and splashed into their quiet reflecting pool.

She told him her secret later on — that Robert, their first-born, had been conceived during their rite of passage, against a background of green and gold. They felt like true explorers — witnesses to the work of the gods.

CHAPTER 2

GOING HOME

R on did not see the black Labrador alongside the Interstate, only the sudden blur of its darting in front of the pickup. Instinctively, Ron's shoulders drew back, his hands stiffening on the steering wheel, as he hammered his right boot down on the brake. "Shit!" Ron exploded, as his pickup jerked violently, skidding sideways. "Stupid, God damn mutt!" The rain-drenched Labrador, its ragged tail bolt upright, disappeared into the tall wet grass beside the road. A quiet hissing sound leaked from one of the rear tires.

The Interstate traffic northward to Springfield slowed, as it veered around Ron's truck. Ron pulled off the freeway, as something made a moaning sound, he didn't know what. Up ahead the view was cluttered with red taillights below darker, ominous clouds.

Alone in his rig, hunting for his lugwrench, Ron started to wrestle again with the unpleasant idea of the letter from the state of Oregon.

Why hadn't his ex-wife contacted him directly if she needed money? He could have just worked things out with Wendy directly. Her old man must be behind this. Ron felt his face flush from the anger.

Ron's gut relaxed as he remembered the first day he met Wendy Robbins at a 4-H booth at the Pendleton roundup. A petite blond with perfect, porcelain-like facial features and an engaging smile, she became his high school sweetheart, his first real love. He pictured Wendy in her shorts and flowered blouse seated next to him as they drove past the grassy green and gold farmlands and wheat fields of eastern Oregon, making love for the first time beneath a cobalt blue sky. That was the summer they'd gone drifting on the Salmon River, the summer before he left for Viet Nam. Not knowing if he had gotten her pregnant, he remembered the anguish.

Then Ron's gut tensed again. No bunch of lawyers from the state of Oregon would give him any trouble at all tonight. After all, he had dealt with lawyers before. Ron always felt uncomfortable around Wendy's dad, a suave attorney. Something about his smooth talk and expensive suits and ties made Ron wary.

Ron left Pendleton the fall following graduation, after being drafted, limping back about a year-and-a-half later, his left knee and shin bone shattered in an ambush at the very end of the Tet offensive.

Ron Hathaway got over the injury. But he never healed from his sense of guilt about being sent back early, even if he had been wounded, while his buddies were left to fend for themselves back in Nam.

Ron sat in his old pickup, now, lugwrench in hand, staring out the window.

Slowly, almost before he knew it, the regular click-clack of the windshield wipers resonated, becoming the beat of helicopters, conjuring up far worse demons for him than the letter from the state of Oregon and the troubles he faced with child support and lawyers — and a vision he hoped would never return suddenly burst forth again with such hellish fury that, even now, it sent a cold tremor of fear through him as he sat in his rig. Leo's eyes, his best buddy's torn body was still lying there by the muddy rice paddy of Viet Nam.

He'd told Melissa about the war. She knew about his nightmares. Never really, though, had he confided about the slow motion sights and sounds and noises he still saw. About the ambush. The death.

In time, Leo's lifeless eyes staring blindly by the side of the road came to mean a kind of all-too-thin membrane between life and death, between a living, wisecracking Leo casually turning his head over his shoulder to say something, and pieces of flesh and blood and bone lying helter skelter on the ground. Not even Melissa was privy to this secret terror within him. Ron had relived the nightmare with only one other person — but the liquor he consumed to lessen the pain had made him forget.

Two years after his return from the war, he and Wendy Robbins were married. Wendy's decision to attend college two short years after Edward was born seemed so out of place and headstrong to Ron. Their divorce was a bitter one. He struggled so hard to pay his child support. His visits with his boy, sporadic at first, gradually became more regular.

Even though Ed was gone now, Ron's child support obligation had apparently not ended. He thought of the letter and the thousands of dollars of unpaid child support he still faced from his divorce.

* * * * *

The broken white lane divider on the freeway flickered by as Ron felt the cold Willamette Valley wind. He was relieved, having satisfied himself that his rig was no longer moaning. A quick adjustment of the idle screw had made the difference. The wet wind-driven drops pounded the side of his whiskery face through the open window of the cab. The wetness felt refreshing, like being on the river again.

For Ron, the red taillights up ahead transformed themselves back to the nights of long ago, drinking with his buddies in the neon-lit bars of Pendleton. He grinned as he recalled one night when he was arrested for taking a leak in the street outside of a noisy Pendleton bar. He absolutely reveled in the wild parties, especially the drunken bouts and carousing after his short marriage to Wendy.

Ron remembered the sobering reality of sporadic jobs and delinquent child support, about Wendy's dad, the lawyer. The man continually leaned on him. Ron did not need the smug lawyer's sermons. After all, Ron hadn't come home to hear lectures from the lawyer about Ron's responsibilities, when Ron already knew what it meant to protect the lives of his platoon buddies back in the war.

The continual letters and court appearances finally took their toll. Ron began looking for work west of the Cascades, as far away from Pendleton as he hoped he could get.

For Don Karr, Ron's childhood friend who worked at the failing Hathaway Hardware Store in Pendleton, it was time for him to move on with his life, too. Don, five years older than Ron, was a tall red-headed fellow with freckles everywhere. He was working as a guide and outfitter in Portland when Ron paid him a visit one day.

"I finally just had to leave, too," Don concluded. They were relaxing in the small front room of Don's apartment on Division Street, listening to Bob Dylan and looking at Don's drift pictures on the wall or lying around the living room. "The store just wasn't doing well with the big chains comin' in," he reflected. Knowledgeable beyond his years about sporting goods, Ron and his parents had been the benefactors of Don Karr's generosity and enthusiasm for fishing and drifting. "What are you gonna do now?" asked Don.

"I'm just lookin' for work so I can pay my damn child support and keep my ass out of trouble," said Ron, slowly swirling a glass of beer in his hand. "I'm gonna check for work here in Portland, then move south down the valley. Wanna see if they have any construction goin' on." After leaving the war, Ron leapt from apprentice to journeyman carpenter in less than two years. He was proud of his skills.

"Hell, Don, we should put together some good drift trips, don't ya think? Like the old days. Why not?" He knew Don's reaction would be positive, as always. "If I'm gonna find work in the valley, we can drift the McKenzie, or even the Rogue," Ron threw out.

"We'll have plenty of survivor parties," Don added. They both laughed, now, as Ron chugged more beer. As Ron noticed Don sipping a glass of water, he remembered that Don always brought ice water with them on the trips. Nothing quenched a parched mouth better to Ron than those short, gulping mouthfuls of ice water from the big clear plastic container while they drifted the sweltering river canyons. Beer was no substitute.

"Speaking of survivors, you remember that little kid we pulled out of the tailings at 'The Queen' below Eagle Cap that one summer? You remember, don't you — the old lode mine in the Cornucopia mining district?"

"Jesus, I'll never forget that," said Ron. "Scarier even than any capsize we'd ever had river drifting. Wasn't that the little Johnson girl?" Ron asked.

"Yeah, Melissa always was a little imp. God, what a wild little animal. Met the Johnsons before I left. They told me she was just gettin' ready to graduate from the University of Oregon in Eugene. Couldn't believe my ears."

"How old would she be now?" queried Ron.

"In her early twenties, I guess," Don replied. "Her folks told me she's working evenings at The Duck Restaurant and Lounge. Should drop in on her, Ron, when you're down that way."

"Yeah. Well, old fella, we'll certainly put some drift trips together when I find work. I need that excitement, that adrenaline rush again," added Ron. Don smiled. They both laughed.

Ron was intrigued right off by Don's casual mention of that kid. Couldn't figure out why, though. Perhaps it was simple curiosity about small town folks he'd known. Perhaps it was more.

Then he remembered how the harrowing ordeal with Melissa had made him never forget this little girl. It was the first time in his young life he felt the pandemonium which inhabits the body when harm, and perhaps death, stalks someone close.

It had been a bright, sky-blue August day in the Wallowas, when everyone returned from a bone-tiring hike to Pine Lakes in the old Cornucopia mining district just south of Eagle Cap Peak, where the Middle Fork empties into the West Fork. The trail rambles for miles on end up through deep old growth, mostly larch and spruce, winding on up through the pine forest of the West Fork Pine Creek Valley. Near the top, the old hard rock Queen Mine burrows into the mountain. They all called it "The Queen." Closed since the Second World War, this gold and silver lode mine had been visited by many local folks.

Suddenly, Connie made a pronouncement. Melissa, barely eight years old, had been missing for some time. A thin woman, Connie was nervous and talkative. A smoker, she seemed to constantly worry, continually in a turmoil over her kids. It was funny to Ron, because Connie's laid-back husband, Ben, seemed such a comic counter-balance to his wife.

"Oh my God, she's gone!" cried Connie. "Where did you last see her?" It was nearing sundown and the long, low shadows were starting to turn the summer mountain air chilly.

"Oh come on now, Connie. She's runnin' around here somewhere," Ben replied nonchalantly. A tall, lanky Swede with an unruly crop of auburn hair, nothing seemed to faze him. "Probably out yonder playin' with some little critter she picked up on the trail," he added, trying to reassure his wife.

"Oh please, I think she's lost! When's the last time you saw her?" Connie asked Ron's dad. A tall, rail-thin man, Ron's dad was sporting a John Deere cap barely containing mountains of coal black hair and was leaning against an old spruce tree, gulping a beer. Intently studying the campfire, he held a metal poker in his left hand, posed and ready to use on the next log which dared to smother his fire.

"I dunno," he began lazily, seemingly unconcerned. "I think she was with us when we passed the old lode mine on the other side of the hill."

What a mischievous kid, Ron thought. A real nuisance. Her unpre-dictable wanderings always earned her many curses from her mother. One minute she would be clambering up over boulders, the next climbing up unexplored streams and pathways, finally dancing out over exposed hilltops and cliffs. She was forever poking around old abandoned lode mine shafts, with their rotted timber beams and their steep tunnels and adits, running back, anxious to show them all her discoveries — rickety wheeled cars, rusted sifters and grinders, and assorted gadgets. This time, though, she hadn't come running back. Reflecting for a moment, Ron felt the night air grow chill. The forest was growing dimmer and his casualness began turning to apprehension.

They had hiked by one rather precarious place on their way back, several miles from the camp. It was the old abandoned mine they had visited several times in the past near "The Queen." Everyone had seemed interested in the old lode mine that was perched high up on a sheer cliff on the other side of the hill across from their trail. But this time everyone was worn and they decided not to take the old miners' trail which led up that way.

"Oh, God, Oh dear God! I know she's been killed, I just know it!" Her mother was now hysterical. "Jesus, Ben, don't you remember! We lost our dog three years ago up near that mine. There was a cave-in. God, that's where there's an opening just above the cliff!" Connie was now standing above the others, waving her arms in a frenzy.

"Yes, that's the one. I think we should go look there first," said Betty Hathaway. She got up from the campfire and headed for the Hathaway tent. A large woman, Ron's mother was always a calming influence.

"She never minds me! She's always running off the trail, just like a wild animal," cried Connie, motioning everyone to get up too. "Damn her anyway!"

"Ron, go get your backpack and flashlight," directed Ron's father, setting his half-finished beer and poker next to the old spruce. "Don, why don't you go with Ron." Don Karr, feeling the cold bite of the high mountain air, suggested that they wear warmer clothing.

Ron, just barely eighteen, got up slowly with Don. His legs and feet were sore. He was tired. Ron felt the night air grow colder as he drew the hood of his warm sweatshirt over his head. Ron really didn't know what to expect to see with the flashlight. Would the beam reveal this little girl's broken body lying at the bottom of a rock-strewn cliff? Or would he see, instead, an immense rock avalanche? They walked back along the trail toward "The Queen." They slowly picked their way up the miners' path directly towards one of the old lode mine entrances at the edge of the 150-foot cliff over the hill.

The climb exhausted Ron. In the three hours since he and Don had left camp that evening, the night air shifted from chilly to shivering cold. It was pitch dark. Ron tried to visualize what the little girl had worn hiking that day. No amount of searching in and around the entrance to the mine or peering over the cliff seemed to give them a clue. He heard the others, who followed the trail farther back, occasionally shouting encouragement. Their voices and shouts faded away.

Ron knew real dangers might be lurking for a young child out here at this abandoned mine. Reaching the top crest above one of the mine's entrances, he suddenly lost his footing. Catching himself, he looked down into a black void — one of the large vent holes which let in air far below. Terrified, he immediately climbed further up the hill above the mine's opening. Several more holes appeared. One misstep, and Ron would plummet fifty or seventy-five feet down into the tunnel.

"Oh God, Don, I think she's fallen in through one of these vent holes!" Ron screamed back down to his friend.

Don, now at the entrance, immediately cast his powerful beam inside. "Com'on down. Let's check it out!" Don replied. "She might'a gone inside for shelter from the cold."

Ron clambered back down the face of the hill above the entrance to the mine. He rushed into the mouth, where broken, damp timbers were strewn about among boulders and rusty, damaged equipment. Walking deliberately, Don continued on ahead, shimmying in about seventy-five or a hundred feet past the opening. He found no clue. Ron suddenly whirled around at the flutter of an escaping bat. The light from his lamp struck a rusted car lying on its side next to even rustier rails. The thought hit him. "Yes, by God, she's gone after some mining equipment," Ron said aloud.

Then he remembered something which unnerved him. Years ago, the miners had left abandoned equipment down near the slag piles at the base of the cliff.

The climb down was precarious. And the pitch-black night offered no clue.

Half an hour later they had wearily inched their way to the bottom of the precipice. Finding themselves at the bottom, they began to doubt whether they would make it back to camp that evening. Ron nervously swung his lamp around, the beam circling the boulder strewn area in a wide arc, glancing off an occasional gnarled pine tree and pieces of contorted and rusted metal cast haphazardly amongst the slag. He was about to suggest that they find a clearing to build a fire and spend the night.

"Hey, peek-a-boo, Ron," came a screechy little female voice. "C'mere you guys!" she yelled at the top of her lungs. "Look what I've found!"

"'Lissa, for God's sakes! You little imp! Do you have any idea what you have done — the trouble you're in?!" Ron yelled with all the strength remaining in his tired body.

Ron laughed aloud, now, in his rig as he remembered cursing and screaming her name over and over again when he saw her little form safe among all those pieces of rusted mining equipment. Her folks always referred to her afterwards as "that little imp." He and Don finally got her back to camp just before midnight. All the way back, to fight off the biting cold and fatigue, they sang together. Woody Guthrie came to mind: "Roll on Mighty Columbia." Then Waylon Jennings. Waylon had that certain dangerous unpredictability about him that appealed to Ron. Just like Melissa.

* * * * *

Part of Ron Hathaway's mind slipped back, now, to the highway leading to Springfield, as the rain slid down the windshield between wiper swipes. He pictured Melissa, again, that rainy night when he walked in on her at work in Eugene. Having just entered his thirties, he really had no idea what to expect from the "little imp" he had known in his teens. Now she was working as a waitress. He would never forget that evening.

"What's the best thing you've got on this menu, young lady?" he asked. Ron seemed to ignore everything as he pulled himself into a booth next to a window. He was hungry. He quickly buried his face in the folds of the large, plastic menu. Ron glanced at the pouring rain outside. He had just finished landing a job with a construction company in Eugene. Even though he was soaking wet, he was in a celebrating, house building mood. He felt confident. Thoughts of Wendy's father and of the mountain of back child support he owed were left far behind. His new job meant he could start paying support for Edward again — maybe that would keep Wendy's old man off his back. He decided now would be the opportune time to check in on that little girl he knew from so long ago. But Ron wasn't sure she was even working this particular weekday evening.

"What's the matter, can't you make up your mind?" came the sweet female voice. Ron took the menu out of his face and glanced up. Her deep hazel brown eyes had a penetrating, knowing look. He was flustered by the eyes. They seemed to reach deep within him. He felt his knees touch the underside of the table as he leaned back.

"Oh, excuse me," he exclaimed, fumbling for words. His eyes dropped from her's to her name tag. "Melissa" it said. He felt his heart start to hammer. He didn't notice that his mouth had left a gaping hole in his face.

"Well, fella, whatta you waiting for?" she teased. He took in her freshly pressed orange and white waitress outfit. It was placed smartly on the young woman. Her long arms ended with beautiful fingernails. She was holding an ordering pad in one hand and a pencil in the other. He cast a furtive glance below where her skirt ended. He had never beheld such long, beautiful legs. Embarrassed, he glanced back up into her eyes, his mouth still hanging open.

"Cat got your tongue? Well?" she chided, now half amused at this man, all wet, sitting in a booth at her area, mouth wide open with nothing to say for himself.

Ron gasped inside. Such an impish little girl, a regular tomboy — someone who had never really been cowed by him at all. His heart pounded with such force that its tempo exceeded anything he'd ever experienced all those years drifting with Don. His baritone voice seemed to almost squeak.

"Ah-hh, ah, are you by any chance little, ahh, 'Lissa...," he paused.

"Boy, guy. You're really out of sorts tonight, aren't ya," she teased again as she nodded at him, rolling her hand as if to coax the thoughts from him. He was soaking wet. He could feel the warmth from his blushing.

"...Johnson. Are you 'Lissa Johnson from Pendleton?" he finally got out. His heart was still pounding.

"Why, yes," she said, looking surprised and a little perplexed. "How did you know who I am?" she added, taking a step back.

"Ever hear of Hathaway Hardware Store in Pendleton," said Ron, again summoning the courage to look directly into those deep hazel eyes which penetrated so deeply into his.

"Oh my God in heaven! Ron!" she cried, placing a hand to her lips. The look of recognition which crossed her widened eyes brought forth a deep, rosy blush, accompanied by a wide smile from her lovely, full lips. He never forgot that smile. Then her arms were around him, her head, her long soft hair pressed next to his, both of them laughing.

Melissa seemed to melt the hard thoughts of Ron Hathaway's past away. He thought of her constantly. Other women reminded him of her. He wanted to share every thought, every experience with her. It was her eyes that did it. Those, and that beautiful, impish smile of hers.

He knew they'd be lovers the second he laid eyes on her. Her eyes captivated his heart. Her beautiful legs stirred a passion that had long been dormant.

Melissa reminisced about how the pursuing smoke from the bright Wallowa campfires caused Ron to "dance about like a wild firefly at night." Together they laughed and sang a lot. And they drifted the McKenzie and, later, the Deschutes River with their friend, Don Karr.

They were married within a year at her folks' Lutheran church in Pendleton. Don Karr was best man.

* * * * *

As his eyes focused on the Interstate ahead, Ron Hathaway's grip on the steering wheel tensed. He pressed harder on the gas pedal. When he and Melissa first settled in Springfield, a working class town sandwiched between the McKenzie and Willamette rivers, Ron worked in construction and his wife taught second grade in neighboring Eugene. The mounting bills and endless summonses to pay his child support pressed down on them relentlessly.

Then there was Melissa's second pregnancy and miscarriage. Ron started drinking heavily. The same thing had happened to his dad with the failure of the family business. But the birth of Joshua, their special child, changed all that.

Josh's hyperactivity consumed them both, especially Melissa, who quit her teaching job. Ron could never quite understand the "diagnosis": Attention Deficit Hyperactivity Disorder — ADHD. It sounded completely foreign to him. All Ron knew was that Josh squirmed a lot and fought to get his thoughts out to Robert and his parents. The boy's painful, contorted gestures and explosive outbursts told Ron that he could not lose it with this kid like he sometimes did with Robert. And the experts could never quite agree on how best to nurture Josh.

Young Robert, a bright, sensitive youngster, was always focused on one interest or another—first dinosaurs, then model planes and cars, and now, at the age of twelve, computers, basketball and piano lessons. And fighting with his brother. When Ron was busy, he took his boy on weekend excursions to his construction sites. Like his mom before him, Robert enjoyed playing among the rigs and machinery.

For Ron and Melissa, there were the weekends. The Friday nights. Melissa loved to dance.

Suddenly Ron's thoughts were cut short by the uneven bumping from one of the rear tires. His steering wheel was lurching to the left. The downpour was steady.

"Damn it!" The ever present curse of his ancient rig.

CHAPTER 3

THE LETTER

He wheeled his old pickup into the double-treaded dirt driveway which entered his property. Tall, dark evergreen fir trees stood in clusters on either side, swaying gracefully. Maybe because of the flat tire tonight, he felt his rig and his two-story seventy-five-year-old wooden Springfield home really went together. He was as fond as a parent of both.

Ron liked the way his rig hummed down the road. He remembered when he purchased it from a fellow in Springfield who had placed an ad selling a "late 1970's Ford pickup in mint condition." Ron smiled at the thought that twelve years later, over 200,000 miles and through one rebuilt engine, he'd kept his truck running. Now the dark blue from the paint job was faded, worn and dusty and pockmarked with gray patches, the chrome fenders scratched and rusted, the front end and roof of the cab dented. He must finally get two new rear tires, or at least retreads. Maybe he'd run down to Mosby's garage this weekend. Mosby always seemed to know where to get parts for his old truck.

Ron listened intently to the low moan as he switched off the engine. Glancing up, he noticed how the black clouds glided slowly, contrasting against the old rusted brick chimney on top of the steeply-pitched roof of his turn-of-the-century farm home.

There hadn't been time to plant too many trees or do much landscaping. The quilted yard of different grasses needed constant weeding. His watchdog Prowler's barking reminded him that he hadn't finished the dog run out back. The German shepherd was pawing the driver's door. Ron grinned at the thought that perhaps this weekend he might enjoy the mundane task of digging post holes and building a fence, though he liked building decks more. He had built Melissa a huge redwood deck out back, off the kitchen door. Now he was getting her ready for a hot tub. The thought always reminded him of that day they had shared by the shaded pool.

Ron was tired. The comfortable kitchen with old-fashioned wall paper smelled of half-burnt pizza. He slid his lunch box down next to his stained Caterpillar hat on the kitchen table he had made from sturdy oak pieces. Glancing down, he noticed that one of his grimy shoes had become unlaced. He went back outside, leaving his shoes on the redwood deck. Reentering the kitchen, he heard the glass from the kitchen window rattle. The leaves had become scampering hands in the breeze, scratching as if to get in.

"You finish your piano lesson? Where's Mom?" he asked Robert in rapid fire succession. He grabbed playfully for the top of his youngster's head, full of brownish auburn hair.

"Dad, she's in the bedroom and needs to talk to you," replied the boy, an urgency in his voice. Robert rushed past him on the way outside, carrying a frayed shoebox — his current secret little project.

Ron glanced at the aged cherrywood piano next to the far end of the living room, satisfied that Rob had taken his lesson. Sheet music was strewn all over the floor and the cloth-covered antique piano bench. Then he noticed the open envelope on the edge of the oak kitchen table. It was marked "State of Oregon - Department of Justice."

"Shit!" he mumbled under his breath. "After all this time." The jolt of seeing the official looking envelope seemed to strike at him like the iron campfire poker his dad wielded so expertly, whacking the smoking logs on those camping trips so long ago. "Piss on 'em," he said aloud. He felt the veins on the back of his hands and neck pulsate. Ron grabbed the envelope and walked briskly toward the stairs.

Glancing up from the envelope, he finally noticed little Josh standing on his head on the dining room couch as he passed. His He-Men and toy soldiers were meticulously arranged in a magical T-formation on the gray green carpet. Josh was exploding and waving his hands at some imaginary creature that only his hyperactive mind could behold. Like a little whirlwind, Josh jumped down and spun around, all in one motion. Ron stopped in his tracks. Josh stared — eyes ablaze — at his dad. He had piercing wide eyes. He exploded with his mouth, and danced around his toy soldiers. "Curr-Booom-Blam," he uttered, his cheeks puffed out. Simultaneously, his hands flew out amid wild facial contortions and body gyrations. His father bent down, gathered him together, and gave him a hug.

The dark, wood-paneled door was ajar as Ron approached their upstairs bedroom. Melissa was seated on the bed with her back to the door — she was wearing the white blouse and pretty blue skirt he liked so much. Her long, auburn hair rested on her slender shoulders. Her hand was touching the bedspread beside her, fingers next to the paper. He went to her and touched her hair.

"I know, 'Lissa. I'm late. Had to change a damned flat. Did you find a babysitter, honey?" he asked politely. "We're gonna have to scramble." Ron anticipated a quick shower as he glanced out the window at the rain which now began to pelt again. A half-empty perfume bottle with the cap off sat on the antique dresser next to Melissa's delicately chiseled walnut jewelry box. The sweet, rich smell of her "Secret Rose" scent reached him and he stroked her hair again. He always bought her that perfume. Glancing back at the mirror, he caught Melissa's frown, her downcast eyes, and returned to her hand, now holding the paper.

"Ron, what is the meaning of this — what is happening?!"

"Oh, those damn gumshoes still want to squeeze blood from a turnip, don't they, hon?" Ron bounced back. "We always seem to be the butt of their computer jokes even after we call them and tell them what the error was. We ought to send Rob down — he'd teach 'em how to fix their screwy computers."

"That's not what this is about," protested Melissa.

"Oh, sure it is, 'Lissa. Shit, those bureaucrats just knew they had to get this letter to us on Friday, the very evening we're plannin' some fun!"

"Ron, this is serious. They say you have a child."

"Bullshit! They're always saying that Ed is still a child. Dammit, 'Lissa! He's gone, now, for chrissakes."

"Stop it!" Melissa screamed as she whirled around. "Just stop it! My God, Ron, look at these papers. I can't believe this! They say you have a fifteen-year-old child! What the hell is going on, Ron," she exclaimed. Her eyes, glistening, now flashed directly into his.

His eyes caught hers.

Ron turned away from Melissa's piercing look toward the bedroom window. A spider was vainly trying to escape at the top of the window, its legs questing and thrashing about. Josh was scared to death of them. The spider clung to one silver strand. The white window trim had started to crack and peel. His glance returned to the dresser. Missing was the familiar sight of a red or white candle in the holder on the old dresser. Melissa always put one there right beside her open jewelry box on Fridays — their secret signal. Had she forgotten this time? Ron did not see Melissa's sudden, thrusting approach. Now the papers were in front of his face. He flinched.

"Ron, what the hell is going on?" she cried again. Melissa disappeared from the room. He looked at the papers, now. His heart pounded and thumped in a strange piercing rhythm as frightening, bold-lettered words appeared: "Mother of the child born out of wedlock." "Obligee-parent — Linda Aguilar." "Obligor-parent — named in the administrative proceedings to establish paternity — Ronald Hathaway." "Name of the fifteen-year-old child: Samuel Whitman." "You owe $26,000 in back, accrued state debt paid by public assistance on behalf of the obligee-mother and child."

The fierceness of the letter's words overcame him, grabbing him in a crushing cataclysm of cold river whitewater — he shivered. His raft had overturned and the current was pushing him down, deep below and underneath the raft. Now, completely helpless, all he could feel was the cold, swift and raging river — a current gone wild — drowning him in the coldness of things he could not comprehend.

Struggling for some kind of foothold, he tried to overcome the sinking. Then the brutal words appeared again: "A fifteen-year-old boy named Samuel." The dark, neon-lit past he had shared with his buddies in Pendleton in the bars, at the parties, flashed — a dark-haired girl had often been there.

"Oh Jesus," he uttered out loud. It was that first name — Linda — and the child's surname, sending a sudden shudder, a pounding in his head, a weakening of his knees.

Ron had known a Linda Whitman his entire life. They had grown up together. She was an Indian girl. Ron stared at the spider and mouthed the girl's name — Linda Pawlik Whitman. Her stepmother, an attractive young Hispanic woman, and Linda's dad, had lived with their large family in an old tar paper-roofed house on the town's outskirts, on a dirt road.

He stood in the middle of the bedroom. He became lost as he stared at the folds of the white chiffon window curtains. His eyes returned again to the spider, now almost halfway down the paint-cracked window pane. It was still swinging to and fro from the end of its slender thread.

Ron thought of the price his father had paid for his heavy drinking. The failed business. It had killed him. Like his father, Ron had taken the same escape in those days. The parties were all a blur. The drink had all but erased his memories of Linda.

He groped for an explanation, an answer for Melissa.

Ron stood next to the bed, paper in hand, paralyzed, stunned. The will to move — to even breathe — had left him. He tried to think of Tate Creek. But he couldn't. The waters of that warm, shadowy pool hidden from the Rogue were lost. A dark, spiraling depression pulled him down, down, down in endless circles of questions with no answers.

That weekend became a murky, cloudy fog, blurring his family. Over and over again the dark-printed words from the letter kept reappearing: "You have thirty days to file a denial of paternity. You must submit to a blood test. If found to be the biological father, you must pay $26,000.00 in past state debt plus current support for the child." The imperious commands seemed so detached and hostile, rubbing like sandpaper across his every conscious moment.

The drive to Drain that following Monday morning was consumed with thoughts of Linda Whitman. When they'd gone to high school together in Pendleton, she'd been slightly plumpish, with long, coal black hair, high cheek bones and a prominent nose. She seemed older to him then, more aloof, more in the company of older guys. When she drank with them, her loud brashness would put him off. Pregnant with her first child during her junior year, she dropped out of high school without graduating. Ron noticed Linda more after the war. What had become of her?

Slowly those times in Pendleton began weaving together — the bars, the party scenes and the drunken "bedding of the wenches." He smiled dimly to himself as he recalled how this silly phrase was bandied about with such cowboy bravado by the collection of his friends known affectionately as "The Raunches." The war and his divorce had reduced him to this, he decided. But mostly the war. Strangely, the thought that had always comforted him the most in Pendleton, to know that the death he had seen justified a detachment from others, especially women, comforted him no longer. He could treat women back then with a sexual abandon which seemed admirable to him for its own sake. Now he had the letter.

Fifteen years! Jesus, thought Ron, goddamned bureaucrat waits fifteen years!

"Hey, Ron," one friend at work kept saying, "they caught you with your sperm in the hatchery, again, didn't they?" Ron felt more anger than amusement at such stuff. Resentful, he drove his rig alone for miles on end. Once admonished by his foreman for leaving the construction site, Ron didn't care. His old pickup became his refuge.

The detached bureaucratic words kept up their relentless, pulsing onslaught: "If found to be the father, you must provide health insurance coverage for the child and the obligee mother if such coverage is available through your employer."

Ron saw Josh's wild-eyed face, his contorted looks and gyrations. Josh's attention deficit hyperactivity disorder worried Ron. But the little boy had bigger problems. "Learning disabled" was the other label he had heard the "experts" use. Ron didn't really understand what Josh needed. "Shit," he seethed to himself, "I can't even get coverage for Josh's problems. How in the hell am I gonna do this, provide all this insurance crap for this new kid, for chrissakes?" Pressing down harder on the gas pedal, he wanted to keep driving past Springfield, right out of the state.

The coldly printed phrase "Automatic Withholding Provisions From Your Paycheck" crushed in on him. "There goes all my goddamned money at Dahlberg and maybe my job," he muttered, cursing aloud as his grip tightened on the steering wheel.

Unnoticed, his truck weaved over the road. "Boss's wife just hates doin' the paperwork on those garnishment things. Cost Randy his job last year. Jesus Christ almighty — are those bastards gonna want my balls, too?!" Ron yelled to himself, his eyes bulging.

The drive in his rig up Interstate 5 continued. Ron tried to climb out of his personal abyss. He had escaped Wendy's old man by disappearing from Pendleton. Maybe that was it. He'd just disappear again.

Pressing his lips ever more tightly together, Ron Hathaway slowly shook his head. The slippery rope ladder dangling from the rock cliff seemed terribly frayed. He was afraid it would break.

CHAPTER 4

THE MYSTIC CHORDS

From an early age, Ron Hathaway learned that Albert Sidney (Sid) Hathaway, his great, great, great grandfather, was a gutsy man. Albert Sidney's father had been a fur trapper and trader along the Missouri River, early in the nineteenth century. He had taken a young Indian woman as his wife, the daughter of a lesser Mandan chief. Her name was Whispering Hawk's Feather. Albert Sidney was the oldest of their six children.

Anxious to see the mighty Columbia River, Albert Sidney sold his dry goods business in Indiana in 1849, outfitted a Conestoga and with his young wife, Clare, and son, joined a wagon train to the Oregon Territory in 1850. They reached the settlement of The Dalles in the spring of 1851. They liked what they saw, especially the wide open and rolling grassland country east of The Dalles.

But Sid wanted to explore farther. He decided to float down the thunderous Columbia whitewater to its confluence with the Willamette River and then travel on down to Oregon City. Clare protested. Sid won out, and his wife agreed that she and his son would remain with friends in The Dalles. His victory almost cost him his life. Shortly after leaving, Sid was pitched overboard in the Short Narrows below The Dalles and nearly drowned. After a stormy fall and winter in Oregon City, Sid finally decided that eastern Oregon would suit his family better. So he mule-packed from Oregon City up through the Barlow Trail's rugged Mount Hood-Cascade route, meeting oncoming settlers, finally reuniting with his family in the spring of 1852.

The Hathaway family remained in The Dalles until the early part of the 1860's when Sid moved the family to the settlement of Pendleton. There, they helped to settle this small town which stood right in the middle of the homelands of the Cayuse, Umatilla, Walla Walla and Nez Perce Indians. Sid was determined he would restart his dry goods business there. Sid was a stubborn, hard driven young man, always going against the current. Maybe that was because his dad had been a maverick and his Indian mother knew how to survive. Ron felt that he had somehow inherited a penchant for river drifting — and an instinct for overcoming the odds — from Sid's Columbia whitewater expedition so long ago.

Melissa Johnson's Swedish ancestors were all devout Lutherans. They had traveled to Pendleton later from Minnesota, in the 1890's, when the area was incorporated and expanding from stock raising to wheat growing. The two pioneer families stayed in Pendleton, helping to build and operate its flour and woolen mills, grain elevators and canneries.

Everyone in Pendleton knew Ron's folks as regular down-to-earth people. That is probably why their business did so well when Ron was young. Everyone knew the name "Hathaway Hardware Store."

At first operating the family's old, established dry goods center, the Hathaways diversified and expanded it into a hardware and sporting goods center, catering to the hunters and sportsmen of eastern Oregon. As an only child, Ron spent many hours at the store, showing the townsfolk the fishing tackle, tents and drift boats. Growing up in Pendleton — with folks who owned and operated a centerpiece store — was anything but tedious.

The Johnsons, small wheat farmers, became good friends with the Hathaways. Betty, Ron's mom, possessed such a vibrant, earthy wit which seemed to lift everyone's spirits, including her husband's. This came hardest, though, when his father drank. Like his ancestor Sid, Ron's father carried a stubborn, rebellious streak — didn't really give a damn what others thought. Ron admired his father, despite what he referred to as "my ol' man's warts."

Ron remembered the best times he spent with his dad, drifting and fishing for brook and Rainbow Trout along the Grande Ronde River in northeastern Oregon. On reaching the takeout point of the tiny isolated town of Troy, they told fish stories and other tall tales at the old Troy Café.

But it was at the opposite end of the state, on one or two occasions with his dad, where Ron learned the secrets of the Owyhee River, a denim blue chord burrowing through the curving walls of jagged and pock-marked canyons streaked with basalt. Golden cornbread plateaus and steppes framed the more distant stone hills, rusted a salmon color by the sun.

Ron never forgot the places he and his dad stopped to see the ancient Indian petroglyphs. "How did these paintings get way out here?" the wide-eyed boy asked his dad.

"I reckon folks from long ago came here to worship," his dad explained. "They painted the animals because they were sacred. The people thought this secret place would protect their paintings."

Ron imagined being there, watching the ancient artisans carefully, slowly carving and painting their treasures into the rocks.

The really special times for Ron, though, were when the peaks of the Wallowas with their alpine lakes and waterfalls, sparkling amidst thick grand firs and Ponderosa pine, beckoned to the whole family. The never ending trails zigzagged ever higher into the Eagle Cap Wilderness, heartland of the Wallowa-Whitman National Forest.

Ron hiked into Sunshine Lake for the first time with his dad at the age of ten. It was a cloudless August morning. The summer snowmelt had cleared the trail. It seemed to Ron like their small group had been climbing up the trail through the Lakes Basin for an eternity.

Like a mirror, the emerald lake reflected the rugged milky white granite peaks of the Eagle Cap. There, Ron was introduced to the mountain hemlock and alpine parklands covered with wildflowers, where bracken meadowlands and grassy fields nestled below majestic snow-capped peaks. From the trails, he and his dad would spot mule deer, elk and an occasional bobcat or eagle guarding the wilderness.

On the way back down to camp, the tired boy stumbled. Glancing up as he caught himself, Ron beheld the graceful freedom of two eagles circling high above, outlined by a cloud hovering near the 9,572 foot high Eagle Cap. Ron stopped and watched the huge outstretched wings floating effortlessly as both eagles soared and dipped, turned and dove. Ron came to think of this place more as his own kind of personal secret, a special kind of treasure even more sacred than the rivers he cherished so much.

There were the really remote places, where his dad took him by horseback to see the fossilized remains of sea creatures and the flat ocean shells embedded high up on the slopes of the limestone hills and mountains. Through the eons, the earth gods had lowered their shoulders and pushed the Pacific seabed eastward, crumpling the land and creating this jagged snow-capped wilderness. To Ron, the creatures' remains became part of his inner secret about this place — as mysterious as the Wallowas' ancient inhabitants, the Nez Perce, had been.

Ron thought again of the Indian girl — Linda Pawlik Whitman — and her family. His folks had told him that the whole area of the Wallowas had been her ancestral home — that the Nez Perce Indians were driven out by the U.S. Army in 1877. The high meadows had served as grazing grounds for the Nez Perce horses every summer. Joseph, their Chief, took his people on a thousand mile chase ending in the snow, in the wilderness, and in disaster for their way of life. Now the large boots of increasing numbers of Anglo hunters, backpackers and sportsmen tramped through the Nez Perce homeland.

As a youngster, hiking along the shaded trails and through the alpine meadows, Ron often wondered if the Indian spirits had ever come back. Would they think Ron a trespasser or would they welcome him?

One day, more out of curiosity than anything, Ron walked up the small hill to the grave site of Chief Joseph's father — his name was Old Joseph — next to Wallowa Lake. Something happened to Ron that day. Standing before Old Joseph's stone column, he imagined how Whispering Hawk's Feather must have lived off the primitive land. Through his Mandan ancestor, Ron felt a closeness — an undeniable kinship — to Old Joseph, giving him a new respect, almost a reverence, for this place and its former inhabitants.

His favorite Wallowa stream, dancing down the mountainside from the Upper Lakes Basin Area, was the west fork of Wallowa Creek, a little south of the town of Joseph. Hiking along a path with a twenty pound backpack one August afternoon, Ron — dazzled — marveled at how the sunlight flashed off this stream, crashing off the mountain boulders in layers of gushing, diamond-studded curtains. Glancing down, he saw the clear mountain water flow peacefully past his feet on the trail. Ron wondered where this little stream would end. He decided that perhaps only the Nez Perce knew the answer to that riddle: did the stream end in Wallowa Lake or in the cursed beast's mouth? Legend had it that a Nez Perce brave had chased a cursed beast across the flatlands north of Wallowa Lake. Both had disappeared into the lake's murky depths where, it was said, the creature now dwelt, tasting the outflow from that mountain stream.

Had the Indian boy, Samuel, met the same fate as the Nez Perce brave? Ron Hathaway wondered. Who was this young man? What things had he seen? What demons was he chasing? Would he drown in a different world beneath raging crosscurrents?

Ron wondered how different the world must have seemed to Samuel than it did to his oldest boy, Ed, and his two sons by Melissa.

* * * * *

The first time Ron took his oldest boy Ed drifting, Don Karr organized the trip with Melissa's blessing. Don was primarily a fly fisherman after the fashion of Ron's dad. Don taught Ed how to recognize the perfect holes below the whitewater where he knew the fish hid. He told the boy where the fish would lay their eggs on the occasional gravel along the riverbeds or beneath the giant moss-covered logs lying askew and rotting in the river.

The peaceful and drowsy hours from later drift trips, when they took turns rowing the quiet, stagnant intervals on the Deschutes and Salmon Rivers, meant time with his boy. They shared the intimate secrets of the sparkling rivulets, the back eddies, the whirlpools and the motionless circles of water.

Ron's "Tiger Tub" slid past the silvery gray rock walls of the narrow river canyons. There the river force narrowed and rolled, bounced and sprayed, at first with a low rumble, then with a booming, hollow locomotive roar. The approaching higher class and more dangerous whitewater rapids caused a rising apprehension, a sudden twist in the chest, a tautness at the temples. Ed learned to read where the bluish green "tongue" of the whitewater chute was hidden. With his dad's prompting, he stood on the boat platform and peered at the bouncing, crashing whitecaps in the distance.

Sometimes, the canyon walls narrowed to rows of magnificent stratified rock pillars perilously balanced on end. Cliff-faced formations resembling leaning and squatting stone creatures appeared. Carved by the wind and rain, these monuments bore spirit-names given to them by the Indians or early explorers such as "Monkey Face," and "Hoot Owl Rock."

Often the sandy river banks were dotted with low-lying scrub and gnarly trees, prickly with thorns. Cows or an occasional deer grazed lazily near river's edge, close-in to the covering shade. Gaggles of Canadian geese weaved in and out of the tall cattails and rushes or dove behind the high rocks. From his boat, Don showed Ed where the Canadian honkers swam almost invisibly in the tall, reedy marshes or waddled along the sand or rocky embankments above river's edge. Clearings on the sand dune shores, ideal for wilderness camping, were shaded with fir or pine tree stands resting above on the embankments. These plateaus either abutted the steep rock canyon walls or rolled back to still more open, yellow sun-scorched fields, with grassland cattle feeding grounds lying directly beneath the high-ridged hills beyond. Once, Don pointed high up into the fractured canyon walls, where a scarcely visible eagle's nest was perched. Occasionally they drifted past an osprey nest resting atop a lone pole alongside the river bank.

They all fished together in the early mornings when the sun, with a single raised eyebrow, peeked over the river valley cliffs. It would gradually warm the sand along the Deschutes or John Day river banks till it felt like crumbly oven hotness on the feet. Ron enjoyed climbing high above the twisting white wrinkles of the river with Ed. From the rugged hillsides, they looked down and marveled at how tiny the ferocious whitecapped churning and cresting of the rapids seemed. Evening fishing was even better than morning fishing. The shadows of the steep, rocky hillsides cast a cool shroud upon the camp, like some giant caped monster. They lay down, looking up at the starry cloud of the Milky Way. The air was very still, while the river tumbled in white-water bursts past boulders and sand dune banks, rolling beyond the campsite and on to unseen whitewater they would ride the next day.

Ron never forgot one trip with Ed on the Salmon River. That was the summer they drifted the river when the flow was unusually strong and high. They had decided to chance it anyway.

Standing on the top of his aluminum boat platform, peering out over the edge of the river, Ron knew that the crew was about to begin a harrowing ride down and through "Demon's Drop" Rapids. "Demon's Drop" was due west as the crow flies from White Bird, Idaho, where Chief Joseph had stood and fought the white man's army before his people had been driven from their Wallowa homelands so long ago. With the river this high, "Demon's Drop" was sure to be hungry — a writhing reptilian dragon.

Standing atop his dad's boat platform, all Ed could see were the bouncing whitecaps. Soon they heard the thunder.

As Ron's boat approached sideways, the smooth greenish blue tongue of the thundering reptilian monster beckoned. Boulders on either side formed the demon's wide-mouthed grin. Huge whitewater teeth waited for the tiny boat to enter. Ron gazed past the mouth, only to see the long, rolling back of the animal undulating rhythmically, finally tapering off to smaller ripples 200 yards downstream.

Ron let his boat drift slowly. He still couldn't see the full monstrous drop in the river. A few hundred feet up ahead, Don's boat was waiting to enter the mouth. Ron noticed the gentle water, backed up behind the tongue and the maze of boulders and whitewater, typical for a much more difficult class-IV rapids. Now seated at the oars, Ron felt the boat rock as it entered the gentle roller coaster ride at the top of the demon's tongue into the drop.

Like all experienced drifters, he kept his "Tiger Tub" turned side-ways facing the bank until he knew where the tongue would be and where the force of the water would meet on both sides, creating, perhaps, the greatest roller coaster ride of a lifetime.

Don's boat was still a few hundred feet ahead. With a burst of rotation, Don straightened his boat out and headed down the tongue into the mouth. The waves grew bigger. Don's boat pitched and rolled violently. Ron counter-rotated his oars, backing off from Don's boat, giving Don plenty of leeway. Don's huge eighteen-foot inflatable grew smaller. His boat completely disappeared below a giant roller of a wave. Ahead of him, Ron saw nothing but whitewater.

Suddenly, the tip of Don's boat nosed straight upward towards the sky. It had climbed up the silver center tooth of the behemoth water monster known as "Demon's Drop." The boat stood on end. It paused for a split second, nose vertical at the crest of the wave. Don, perched helplessly at the oars, seemed somehow glued to the back of his boat behind the large cooler in front of him. Ron felt a shiver run through his chest and into his hands. He trembled. Got to keep the God damned boat straight, he reminded himself. His heart was pounding. His hands, wrapped around the ends of his nine-foot oars, were white vice grips. Don's boat, cresting the fifteen-foot tooth of the monster, disappeared into its throat.

"Jesus, Dad! What do we do now?" cried Ed. Ron felt the blood in his head pounding again. He knew, instinctively, that he must keep his sixteen-foot inflatable headed straight into and up over the fifteen-foot rolling water monster.

"Forget the oar!" Ron yelled. Ed wedged the small oar he was gripping into a crack beneath the seat on the boat frame and adjusted the straps on his life jacket. "Get down and lean into the thing," he yelled to Ed above the roar. His son now perched himself in the front of the boat with both knees on the floor. He grabbed at either side of the frame. His head was down as if in fervent prayer.

Ron's boat pitched and lurched violently upward. In an instant the boat spun and slid sideways. His nine-foot port oar was pinned to the side and was now upright. All Ron could see was the blue sky.

"Get down!" he shrieked again, as Ed slid into the bottom of the front and was flung sideways. Ron turned to his right. The breakneck wall of boiling, spraying whitewater so crushed in on him that all became silent, slow motion. Off to his left, the force of the roller continued to slam the boat upward. For an instant, out of the corner of his eye, he glimpsed the river trough below. He was now more than halfway up the Gargantuan silver-toothed roller barrier. The boat heaved again precariously to the left. Then he glanced back up — way up — at Ed in the front end. All else vanished except his left oar and the pounding of his heart. He felt his hat being ripped off his head by the demon's invisible hand. He dropped the right, starboard oar. He flung himself at the left, upright port oar, grabbing it with both hands and pulled with all his might. The boat, now sliding wildly sideways, began tilting upwards. Ron pulled at the oar with a surging burst of adrenaline. Ron sensed his son's body above him, about to fall backwards onto him and the oar.

"Bang!" The jaws of the roaring reptile snapped shut like a vise on the nine-foot oar, breaking it like a small toothpick, the sharp crack and bark of the gunshot echoing. Bent under tons of hydraulic pressure, the heavy oar snapped just as the boat crested to the top of the high-speed, uphill roller coaster. His boat was poised sideways atop the largest of the demon's silver teeth. Ron held the top half of his splintered nine-foot oar in his hands.

He felt himself and the boat drop precariously, nearly vertically, crashing weightless into the mouth of the monster. Just as suddenly, Ed disappeared over the side. Ron lost his breath. His gut flipped and burst upward from his stomach and center into his throat as the boat fell. Ron's mind went blank. His choices were gone. Ed was gone.

Ron noticed the rope coil from the oar spin away into the spray with the bottom half of the oar still attached. Having reached the crest of the monster, the nine-foot oar had held the boat just long enough to allow it to crash-roll the opposite way from the crest, spinning the boat downwards into the water trough, still upright.

"Oar gone! Out of control!" Ron screamed. "Give us a hand, Don! God damn it, my oar's broken! Ed's overboard!" Ron let loose with all his remaining adrenaline. He realized that his boat, minus Ed and its vital oar, was now doomed to be swallowed alive down deep inside the whitewater throat of the monster, then gripped and thrown and twisted mercilessly in its bowels, only to be defecated at the rear end, probably splintered into pieces far down river.

The boat blindly crested the remaining rollers, while Ron crouched in his boat like a helpless squirrel on a rolling log at timber drift time. Finally Ron noticed Ed's head, sandwiched between the faded orange folds of his Mae West life jacket, bobbing like a cork. Don turned his boat towards the bobbing head and extended an oar to an eagerly outstretched arm. Ron waited. After some effort, Don finally pulled and levered Ed and his Mae West aboard.

As Ron approached Don's boat, Ron's raft was now slammed hard against jagged rocks by the swift current, fatal protrusions to an inflatable boat.

Suddenly, there was an abrupt, hollow "Boom," followed by a long hissing. "Oh, Jesus! Don, we've got a blowout!" Ron yelled. Would the boat, itself, or the entire trip now be abandoned? Would they chance overloading Don's boat for a risky drift? Or did this mean a lonely back-breaking hike out of the wilderness? A tear on the bottom of the raft could be fixed quite easily, not like a hiss from a punctured air chamber.

Don, this time pulling his boat over, saw that Ron had forgotten his spare, nine-foot oar. The rapids were behind them.

"Ron, can you tell where the trouble is?"

"Can't tell if its in the outer or middle chamber. I don't think the floor's been torn, though," replied Ron.

"This is going to be a challenge." Don looked serious. They managed to land both boats in a quiet back eddy. Don quietly motioned Ron to come aboard his craft. Ed was seated in Don's raft, shivering, a look of mixed panic and bewilderment still on his face. Don brought out his patching kit and untied the extra oars. Don was a deliberate fellow.

For the next two hours, in the calm back eddy, up on a sand dune embankment, Don and the two survivors patched and used the foot pump to reinflate the damaged chamber on the "Tiger Tub." And they fashioned another length of oar. Ron always marveled at Don's ingenuity. For Don, anything was possible. Don was able to tie and tape two of their smaller, four-foot oars together.

"What a handyman," Ron marveled. "You're quite a creative kind of guy, you know." They both laughed. Ron wondered, though, if the new shorter oar would get him and Ed through the next two days of high-class rapids on the Salmon River.

Breaking his nine-foot oar had left an impression. Ed wanted to leave his dad's boat and drift with Don. For the rest of the trip. Wounded, Ron was taken aback by his son's apparent disloyalty.

Lying awake outside his tent that night, next to a fading campfire, with his arms folded behind his head, Ron stared up at the edge of the Milky Way and worried about facing what might be the first of several sleepless nights. He couldn't forget the gaping mouth and that silver tooth leading up to the drop. Why hadn't he been able to keep his boat straight? "Only the spirits understand, dad." Ed had offered this answer to his father with a weary smile as he entered the tent for a night's sleep.

Old Joseph must've known the "Demon's Drop" and other creatures well — both flesh and stone — and had taught the lesson to his son, Chief Joseph.

The Great Spirit Chief — that's what Chief Joseph had called his vision of God. The Great Spirit Chief had created the land and mountains, the sky, the rivers, and the creatures of the earth. These things were irreplaceable. Without them the earth's children couldn't survive.

This notion made sense to Ron as he gazed up into the starry sky. Joseph would say that the "Demon" was there to test them. All things created by the Great Spirit Chief possess the Great Spirit — a consciousness — which is unique in all the world.

This was the Spirit which Joseph understood. And out of the Great Spirit the Great Chief created the Human Spirit — the spirit of the heart, of the mind. The Human Spirit helps the earth's children listen to the Great Spirit.

Perhaps, Ron thought, listening to the Great Spirit is important before making the choice to commit.

Ron Hathaway decided that once having made the choice to commit, he could not go back up "Demon's Drop" and start over. Such were the other choices he had made in life.

The choice to commit. He repeated the thought. It had cost Leo his life. It had also meant the birth of Ed. The youngster needed commitment from his dad. Yet he had not always been able to give his son a steady oar.

God knew he paid his support when he could find work. But wasn't it really like the pressure from the slowly dying business that had killed his father? After all, he left Pendleton to be forever rid of his father-in-law's ridicule — the constant, self righteous hectoring he resented so much — the continual threat of being eaten alive by wage garnishments engineered by a rotten lawyer.

Ron glanced over at the tent, listening to his son's soft breathing. He slowly shook his head. He knew all the excuses. He smiled. To Melissa, Ed had always been family. It seemed such a natural extension of Melissa's growing up with her two brothers, Benjamin and Adam. They became uncles not only to Robert and Josh, but to Ed as well. They traveled to Pendleton to visit Melissa's family every chance they got. Ed was completely drawn in when Melissa's dad, Ben, and Betty Hathaway mixed their sense of humor. Their campfire stories always left everyone in stitches.

The sharp edge of bitterness had finally worn down with time. The paying of support, sometimes erratic, mostly regular, became more of an involvement with his son, with his life, than a sword thrust into his side. Ron was proud. And he knew he had earned his son's love and respect.

The Human Spirit — the choice to commit — his son's love and respect. The whole idea made sense to Ron, lying there that night by the Salmon. He, alone, must teach these things to his children.

Having decided all of these things, he finally smiled broadly to himself, picked himself up from his spot next to the smoldering campfire embers, entered his tent in the darkness of night and fell asleep next to his son.

* * * * *

The next afternoon, Ed was happily back in his father's boat. At least this was some consolation for Ron. At the confluence of the two rivers, the merging of the Salmon with the majestic Snake, a greater consolation, a kind of regeneration overtook him. And he worshiped it because it gave him a special rite of passage with his son.

In his early twenties now, and a navy ensign stationed in San Diego, Ed still talked of those times.

Later Robert, too, would become a survivor of the whitewater with his dad. During one sudden, turbulent May rainstorm, they leaned over the railing between two side pillars, peering at the blue green Mackenzie flowing under the covered bridge below Gate Creek Rapids.

The slightly pudgy boy looked up at his father and asked, "Dad, how many fish swam under this bridge today?"

"Oh, enough to feed a whole crew of drifters, Rob."

They talked drift stories. They discussed dinosaur and Indian lore. Ron told him about "Demon's Drop." It was like the fright the youngster had felt as their boat crashed through the thrashing Marten Creek Rapids earlier that afternoon on the Mackenzie. Ron taught his son the things he had learned on the Salmon.

Robert loved the passing view of the Columbia River along the Gorge on the way to the Wallowas and the Salmon River. Water spewed from the floodgates, foam gushing from the cement teeth of the giant dams biting into the mighty Columbia. The drive in his rig through the high steppe into Pendleton was sleepy, except when the boredom was interrupted by an occasional dust storm swirling in the distance. The Columbia and the barren harshness of the brown landscape was a reminder to Ron and Melissa of what their ancestors had faced.

At age six, Rob believed all of those wild stories his dad and Don told him about the Indians who lived along the river. The Indians, of course, had lived here long before the white man had come. They had drifted the rivers many times in their canoes. They had hunted for elk and deer and fished for salmon and trout. They had played on the rocks and slides. The red man would not be happy with a child who littered their sacred places. Spirits would come to haunt him.

One bright July midday, they put in at the abandoned Salmon River placer mine just above "China Rapids." The gravel pit ruins and piles bulged from the sides of the grassy hill embankments turned brown by the sun. The huge gray, blue and white rock mounds and tailings ran for hundreds of yards adjacent to the river. A century-old crumbling cedar cabin stood atop a grassy knoll. It had been constructed by the miners and stood as if it was a relic in a museum. Inside were old papers, rusted cans and various colored glass jars — purple, green, blue and shiny red — the birthplace of Rob's Wild West imagination.

Forever curious about what was inside the ancient dwellings along the river, Rob discovered a small root cellar embedded in the hillside behind the cedar cabin. He approached the small door of the cellar. It opened with a squeak. The boy felt a refreshing coolness brush against his face. Suddenly, the empty tin can sound of the tail of a western rattler froze Rob in mid stride.

"Dad! Dad! Ahhh!" cried the boy. Don had gone back to check the pressure in one of the boats. Ron heard his boy cry out. Unconcerned, at first, he became puzzled when the boy started to cry and wouldn't move. Closer, he saw the head of the coiled rattler next to the door not two feet away from the boy.

"Don, rattler! Come quick, Rob needs help!" The boy's fright might provoke the snake.

Ron now tried to reassure his boy. "Just stay put, son. Calm down. Don't move. You'll be all right." They had always carried a first aid and snake bite kit with them.

"Dad, please help me! I don't want to die!" From stories the boy knew the rattler was poisonous. He knew he had trespassed where he shouldn't be. Were the Indian spirits paying him back for some transgression? The rattle went off a second time. The boy trembled.

"Ron, here's a stick," Don said, approaching from behind. Ron took the long stick from his friend's hand. With the end he coaxed and prodded the coiled snake away from the boy.

"Now back up, son," instructed Ron. The boy, too terrified to move, needed a little more prodding. "Go ahead, Rob, back off now." The boy obeyed. The creature disappeared inside.

"Still want to go inside the root cellar and visit the residents, kid?" chided Don. The boy was not laughing.

"That's not funny, you guys!" his face now ashen. He scowled at them both. "Why didn't you kill the thing? You could 'of you know." He had both hands on his hips, just like Melissa always did when she got mad.

"Do we kill critters just because we get in their way? If that was your home, would you want someone coming in unannounced?" Hopefully, his dad's questions might show him that the creature had the right to live another day. The boy was learning his dad's respect for the wilderness. And his mother's sensitivity towards "critters."

Ron never forgot when Melissa, as a kid, had carefully returned from one of her wanderings to their parents' tent-encircled Wallowa campground, holding an injured sparrow in her upturned hands. Her eyes were brightly, tenderly fixed on the bird's broken leg. She nursed the thing back to health and released it later at her parent's farm.

Like his mother, Rob was not deterred from exploring other caches where mining equipment had long been abandoned, with rusted balls and chains and screens, wheeled rigs and contorted, twisted cars over-turned on their sides or standing catywumpus on rusted rail forms. They were all treasures hidden by the outgrowth of tall crabgrass, reeds and scrub trees turned yellow golden and brown under the scorching Salmon riverbank sun. More treasures lay hidden beneath the river. Their presence told Rob of the ancient times when miner adventurers crashed down and through the whitewater rapids with their precious metal cargo lashed aboard flat-bottomed boats. Rob imagined how the boats would occasionally be thrown about and overturned by the treacherous current, sinking to the bottom. The rapids bore the names of the adventures and disasters given to them by those miners: "Devil's Slide," "Bodacious Bounce," "Buckskin Mary," "Snow Hole," "China Rapids," "Bjorkie's Boulder."

Watching his son's excitement when they would stop and explore each new place along the remote river bank, Ron pictured little Melissa at play in the Wallowas. He grew warm.

He thought of Melissa again in the shaded pool beneath the slide on the Rogue. The vision always came to him when he dreamt of the river and of Melissa.

Ron grinned as he recalled that first drift trip they all took together in mid-June down the John Day. Little Josh sat squirming next to his mom on the front seat of the "Tiger Tub." His skinny form, hidden under a billowing yellow Mae West life jacket, was tense with fear. He whimpered and clutched at his mother's neck and arms as they bounced through "Clarno Rapids."

This was Melissa's first visit to the orange red cathedrals of the Great Basalt Canyon of the John Day River. She marveled at the stone pillars which rose hundreds of feet above water's edge, solemn columns scoured black at the water line, bleeding to reds further up, with spires towering high on top, pointing upwards at the gliding clouds. The enormous embrasures and buttresses, with their solid tan and reddish hues, formed the canyon walls. Every so often in the late afternoon, Melissa would catch her breath. With the setting sun lighting the way, Ron's boat became a shoe, floating down the center aisle of a blazing stone cathedral.

The next day Melissa became enamored with the yellow tapestry of the John Day chaenachtis plant blooms, blanketing the low rolling knolls of the Painted Hills everywhere. She was astonished by the hundreds of small openings honeycombing the sand-rock embankment outcroppings. Ron explained that cliff dwelling birds, bank swallows, inhabited these walls.

They pulled the boat around one of the right-way bends in the river, behind a 200-foot stone cliff. Stopping to rest, Melissa and the boys hiked up to the "Hoot Owl Rock" outcropping. Ron stayed below that day. Josh scared Ron by waving his hands wildly at the top and faking a fall off of the other side into the river canyon below.

His little whirlwind, his hoot owl, so wild, yet so sensitive. Seeing such joy and such innocence left Ron sad, though. He wondered if Josh might somehow not make it in the real world.

CHAPTER 5

SEARCHING FOR ANSWERS

Ron turned his pickup slowly off the two-laned asphalt roadway. He was now in Springfield. The old vehicle banged through rain-filled potholes. He parked alongside The Keg Tavern.

"Hey, Landon, how's it going?" Ron was relieved to see short, ruddy-faced Landon Saxton with his arm tattoos. His favorite barkeep was still at work, chattering with customers and wiping down the bar. Landon had been at The Keg ever since the early days when he and Melissa moved to Springfield. There had been long gaps in their acquaintanceship. Ron was glad, though, that Landon was still trying to make a go with the business. While the go-go girls brought in the customers for awhile, problems developed later. Ron had heard that the city council and liquor commission threatened to shut Landon down. Things got too dicey and Landon cut the girls loose. Still, Landon had managed to survive.

"Yo, Ron, good to see ya. What'll it be tonight?" Landon greeted him from behind the glossy top of the wooden bar as if he'd only been there the night before. The go-go stage off to the side was vacant since Ron had seen it last, now circled by tables with an occasional customer seated in one of the metal chairs. A couple of men from a road crew were talking. One leaned back, listening to the lazy strains of a Tex Ritter tune from the jukebox next to the front windows.

"Ah, give me a pitcher," replied Ron. Glancing around, Ron noticed three of his younger co-workers from Dahlberg huddled in a booth, next to one of the velvety green pool tables in back. Monte and Larry, sports aficionados, were engaged in an intense conversation with Randy. Ron was surprised to see Randy Baccus. A stocky, loud carpenter who swore a lot, Randy had left Dahlberg awhile back after his divorce, amid a flood of wage garnishments. The father of two boys, Ron had heard rumors that the carpenter had fallen way behind in his child support payments but somehow had managed to make ends meet. Ron brought his pitcher over to the table.

"Hey, this is a switch, pal," exclaimed Monte Demarco, an outgoing newlywed fellow in his twenties. Monte was proud of his ability to roof a house "faster than anyone."

"Hey, guys. What's cookin?" Ron hesitated, feeling slightly awkward and out of place. A man in his mid forties, it had been a long time. Feeling the weight of his troubles, he was in no particular mood to hear shop talk from lads. Still, he sat down. Ron wanted to know how Randy Baccus had managed since leaving Dahlberg. One or two drinks later, Ron opened up. Larry Craig, a journeyman framer for Dahlberg, talked nothing but sports. They all called him "The Jock." It was Larry who brought up the subject of the letter.

"Shit, I just seem to get screwed every time I think I'm doin' O.K.," complained Ron.

"Now, don't go gettin' moody on us," retorted Larry with a wide grin. "After all, you can always get yourself a good lawyer like Randy did."

"Yeah," chimed in Randy.

"Ah, gimme a break, for chrissakes," Ron said, his face reddening. "All those damned shysters care about is bleeding money out of your wallet! I remember my old man, how pissed off he'd get. Every time he'd need a lawyer when the store got into trouble. They never came through for him. Really messed him up." Ron gulped his beer and looked over at the stocky carpenter.

"Well, my lawyer wasn't too much help with my divorce either, I guess," volunteered the carpenter. "Got screwed. Old lady got the house, the best car and all my money. That son-of-a-bitch judge made me pay $500 a month alimony plus outrageous child support for my two kids. No goddamned consideration for me. Here I am working my ass off and I get royally fucked!" Ron could tell that Randy Baccus was on a roll, now, and he felt a kind of bond with this man, if for no other reason than that they both despised the same thing.

"Sounds like you really got screwed, man," exclaimed Ron.

"Yeah, and that's not the half of it. This shyster I hired to represent me was no goddamned good. In the end, just dropped the ball. Charged me an arm and a leg. Wouldn't answer any of my questions. Never returned my phone calls. A real fuck-up."

"What did you do?" asked Ron.

"Well, shit, my ex-old lady had her lawyer garnishee my wages at Dahlberg. Really pissed me off." Baccus took a high arching swig of beer, bringing his glass down hard on the table. "Then I ran into this friend who knew a fella that was counseling divorced fathers and I went in and seen him. A real smooth son-of-a-bitch. And then I seen this other lawyer the counselor guy sent me to who told me some things I could do to protect myself."

"What happened, Randy?" Ron's feeling of anger towards lawyers was beginning to drain away as he took another swig from his glass.

"Well I sure as shit wasn't gonna hang around here and continue workin' my ass off for Dahlberg. I just up and quit and left the state. Went up to Washington to find work. No fuckin' way was I gonna pay off all that child support. Shit, I owed over $17,000. Besides, the ex turned out to be a real bitch, too. Wouldn't let me see my kids at all."

"That's kind of a shitty thing to do," Monte said.

"Did you try to see your kids?", asked Ron.

"Na, the kids just sided with the old lady all the time. Always whining to me about their mom not gettin' any support. Just decided I'd had it. Decided to pull the plug and watch the bitch get stuck in the drain." They all laughed in a kind of group therapy. Larry Craig got up from the table to fetch another pitcher of beer. They all continued to drink and shoot pool.

Uncharacteristically, Ron's pool game suffered that night, though more out of a brooding than a lack of skill. Baccus really didn't sit well with him. The man's boasting seemed callous, almost cruel. The more Ron drank and lost, the more he brooded.

The brash carpenter had avoided his child support by leaving the state and finding a new job. He exuded a confidence that had escaped Ron. Perhaps Baccus knew something that he didn't.

Ron sat down at the table after losing his final game. He asked the carpenter again what he did after he found work in Washington. Back in Springfield this particular Friday night to visit old friends and to pick up belongings he'd left at his folks place in Eugene after the divorce, the man seemed pretty happy with himself.

"Found a good lawyer in Washington who advised me to lay low for awhile," he stated coolly. Ron wondered how Randy Baccus was supporting his ex-wife and two boys.

"Do you still pay child support?" Ron asked.

"Fuck, no!" he bellowed. "She wouldn't let me see the kids so I got even. Not angry, just even."

"How the hell did you pull that off?" Ron was leaning forward across the table looking intently at his former co-worker.

"Well the guys here been tellin' me 'bout your situation, Ron, so I've figured out how you can screw the system."

"Well, come on, tell us," Ron said, gesturing in a rolling manner with his right hand as if trying to coax the words out of his mouth. The man's cockiness was bracing.

"Just work under-the-table now and get paid cash," Baccus replied with a sly grin. "Anybody gets technical, I just give 'em a fake social security number. The sons-a-bitches will never be able to trace me that way," he ended with a note of contempt.

"Don't you ever see your kids?" asked Monte, the newlywed. "Don't you ever miss 'em?"

"Are you kiddin' me, Monte? 'Course I miss 'em, but I'm sure as shit not gonna rock the boat." He paused, took out a cigarette, lit it and took a long draw, tossing his head back and blowing smoke rings. Returning his attention to Monte, he continued. "I see my kids, and their mother's gonna be after my ass, again, for support. Ain't gonna give the bitch the satisfaction of doin' that to me again," he exclaimed.

Monte glanced down at the table, put off by the man's blast, a look of quiet but polite disgust on his face. Baccus, ignoring the mood, took another deep drag on his cigarette, blowing smoke in Ron's direction.

"I'm telling ya, fella, play it smart and ya won't have any problems either," he emphasized, poking the air with his stout finger as he continued exhaling puffs of white smoke in Ron's direction. "Been stayin' with this real nice broad in Battleground, Washington." Battleground was a long stone's throw up the Interstate from Portland. "Has a kid of her own. A real fox. I get along just fine," he said, smiling and taking a drink followed by another long draw from his cigarette. "Get laid every night."

Ron Hathaway sat at the table, silently drinking and listening to the voices. Thinking about his own boys, especially Josh, Ron wondered if he could put himself in Randy Baccus' shoes. Then the $26,000 burden blew down on him. His temples began to pound.

In his quiet, drunken brooding, Ron lost track of the lawyers, the social security numbers, the jobs he might find out-of-state. He drank more to drown out the relentless onslaught of the state of Oregon, which he knew was about to grab $26,000.00 without so much as giving a damn about his own family.

The music crashed through the table conversation as couples began to dance. He drank some more, much more, and the music and voices faded away. That evening, Ron Hathaway struggled to keep his balance.

* * * * *

Melissa, too, struggled to keep her balance. Ron's drinking, his moodiness, had shaken her. But it had not always been this way.

Early on, Melissa had dubbed his sixteen-foot red-and-black boat the "Tiger Tub." Ron told her the name fit like no other.

Navigating the "Tiger Tub" through the Rogue's "Blossom Bar," they jarred past "The Picket Fence" — a dangerous, granite garden full of traps, twists and turns. Bucking the current, Ron turned his boat hard about among the immense stone monoliths rising in the midst of the thundering Rogue. They protruded like giant fingers of a submerged hand, waiting to grab the boat and its occupants, to crush them in its whitewater fist. They slid past immense gray white boulders rolled there during the Ice Age. Some were bald and smooth, some were as sharp as knives. They stood like statues amid the roar and crash of the mighty current — a monumental Stonehenge crafted by glacial gods long ago.

And that secret place she'd once visited, nestled back inside the Rogue's mysterious river forest, was still rich within the recesses of her mind. She nurtured the memory of her younger tomboy self, sliding on her bottom down the smooth, rock slide into the cold Indian pond, her body meeting Ron's, feeling his smooth, powerful shoulders. For her, the soft, gentle murmurings of the water arching off the end of the slide that dreamy July afternoon signified Ron's new presence in her life. The fingers of sunlight had glistened and danced through the tops of the trees, gently touching the branches and wet moss. It had sprinkled the shadowy water and she felt it soothingly warm her back and legs. This divine place — the drowsy sunlit reflections glancing off the pond where once Indian children had played — seemed to envelop her with its spirit.

Melissa awoke to little Josh's explosions. In front of her he waved his thin little arms and legs. His hands danced wildly above his head, covered with close-cropped brown hair. His dark eyes darted about the room. A cataclysm of verbal explosions flew from his mouth: "Mom, Mom, Mom! Can I have my snack now? Mom, when are my cartoons on? Mom, when are they on? What time is it, Mom? Mom?" The wild motions of his small hands punctuated his demands.

Her little whirlwind needed help in school. There was a meeting scheduled with the school counselors and special education staff, as well as Josh's teachers.

Melissa had struggled with Josh for seven long years, making endless trips to the pediatrician to adjust Josh's Ritalin intake. She noticed that he could focus somewhat in structured settings — mostly at school — but almost never at home. The rest of the time the Ritalin cut away his appetite like a suction tube.

The teachers would scold students who made fun of his not eating at lunch. Josh knew he was different than the rest. He would speak in quiet whispers to his mom about the things which hurt and frightened him the most. He could not comprehend why.

Melissa was only reminded that her husband could no longer cope. Robert seemed forgotten. When Ron drank, his unpredictability and his curtness frightened Rob so much. The youngster would scowl and retreat to his room or outside with his old shoe boxes. He would sit idly by the piano or his computer and ask Melissa, in a feeble voice, "What's the matter with Pop?"

Slowly Melissa tried to help Ron untangle the web of his re-emerging alcoholism and the loss of balance in their lives.

They were both seated at the oak kitchen table late one Friday night in their cozy kitchen. They read and reread the papers. They wondered about the blood tests that needed to be taken. The money. The lawyers. She knew that the difficult questions had to be answered by someone, some nameless, uncaring person. The phone number on the paper bore the same stark reality as Ron's state paternity case number — a salvo of depressing numbers.

"Ron, we've got to get in to see some lawyers before its too late," she sighed. Ron, hunched in his chair, was looking very glum, defeated. "Did you really read these papers?" she asked.

"Jesus, that's all I've been doin' for the past two weeks," he muttered. He took another swig from the quart of beer and continued munching his pretzels.

"Well, these instructions say you've got thirty days to file legal papers with the court. Did you know that? If you're going to deny you're the father, you've got to file papers and find some good legal help." Melissa spoke firmly and slowly, trying to make her words sink in. "If you don't, we're screwed, Ron," she said with finality.

"Well, do you know any good lawyers?" Ron's skeptical look told her he was resisting the idea.

"There might be one in Eugene or Salem. I've made a few calls," she added. Melissa had made a short list of names of lawyers recommended by their neighbor Sharon Gunderson and other friends.

"I dunno, 'Lissa. All those shysters want is your money," he scolded. "They all talk a good line. Those sons-of-bitches never did anything for Pop's business!" Ron scowled. "Christ, all they hollered about was getting paid while Dad's guts were being ripped out!" Ron looked down, a tone of disgust entering his voice. "What are they gonna to do for us, except to bleed us dry, for chrissakes?" Ron took another swig, a look of scorn still on his face.

"It's settled, then," said Melissa with a look of determination. Ron winced. "We're gonna see a few of these lawyers right away and you and I'll make a decision." She searched his eyes for some sign of agreement. Ron's look of skepticism continued, but he nodded. Time was running out.

* * * * *

The call Ron made from Drain during his lunch break one day was followed by a recorded message leading him through a long maze trying to find a real person who might answer his questions. Finally a voice on the other end, a real live female voice — very official — asked him for his case number, name and the name of the mother. Ron knew that he might finally be getting some long-awaited answers.

"What about a blood test, when do I come in?"

"No blood tests are scheduled until a formal denial is filed which must be filed within thirty days after you receive the State's Notice," he was told.

"Do I have to get a lawyer? How much will a lawyer cost me?"

"Yes, you should get a lawyer and no, I do not know how much it will cost you."

Jesus Christ, he thought, what do these people know! And then he thought of Samuel.

"Can I talk to the mother of this little boy, Samuel? Do you know where he lives?" Ron asked plaintively.

The answer from the nameless voice came back: "We do not represent the mother in these proceedings. We only represent the welfare assistance agency which gave public assistance to the mother."

"Well why in the hell am I talking to you, then?" Ron protested, beginning to feel his temples pound.

"Quite frankly, we have no interest in issues involving custody or visitation — only in obtaining child support from the father to reimburse the state agency which has paid assistance to the mother for the child." The voice at the other end seemed distant, metallic, electronic.

A steel door seemed to clang shut in front of Ron.

"Well then, can I at least contact the mother and discuss this matter with her?" he blurted out. "I want to find out about her and the child. What do you know about them?"

"Sorry, we cannot release any information as to the mother or the youngster's whereabouts. Federal and state regulations make these records confidential," the electronic voice replied. He heard the clanging reverberation of another steel door closing, locking him in a prison full of fear and gnawing paranoia.

Memories of his dad's troubles with the IRS, before the family hardware business had failed — before his fatal heart attack — now burst forth with a vengeance. His dad's anguish flashed back — the time the IRS penalty notice arrived at the house, when his dad frantically tried to call the numbers, tried to talk to someone, and couldn't get through. His father's business troubles were finally drowned by liquor. "This is the same old shit Dad had to put up with!" he yelled. These bastards are just like the fucking IRS. The thought went through his mind with such blind fury that he did not notice that he had returned to his rig without hanging up the pay phone.

Didn't Linda know? Everyone in Pendleton knew his parents and could reach him at any time. Why hadn't the state contacted him through his folks? Hell, everyone in Pendleton knew Hathaway's Hardware. Ron's thoughts circled around and around in his mind as he drove his rig aimlessly through Drain. There was only one escape now through the closed cistern-like doors. Drinking made the thoughts go away.

* * * * *

Perhaps the flashing blue and red lights were a wake-up call. Her husband's disheveled appearance and bloodshot eyes at the Eugene police station that night were strangely a relief for Melissa. Perhaps alcohol counseling, through Oregon's drunk driving diversion program, would put him back together. But at what expense? she wondered.

The only way is to tie the poor bastard up and haul him in to see a good lawyer, she thought.

The trips to the lawyers' offices seemed like a parade through expensive rooms with lush carpeted floors and clean, glossy-topped desks and furnishings. The oak bookcases were all stacked neatly with volumes of leather bound books, the walls covered with an array of meaningless, important looking certificates from faraway institutions. The people behind the glossy desks with their suits and swivelling chairs seemed important too, at least to themselves. And so did the fees — $4,500.00 to take Ron's case. Then $7,500.00. Then $10,000.00. The prices rose as the offices and suits became more plush and expensive looking. To Melissa, the highest priced lawyers seemed to display such arrogant airs and to posture so stridently, all the while bragging about big courtroom victories which escaped her ears. Even so, Ron's spirits seemed to brighten at the courtroom war stories. Melissa had to remind him with some heat one afternoon that there was simply no way they could ever get the money to pay the expensive "retainer fee" for the lawyer he wanted.

Up to now, Melissa had been too afraid to admit to herself that she had become the prop for Ron's own weakness. Somehow, she had to change this. Still, she was torn over what to do. She was homesick for the security she knew as a child. Her chronic stomach pains were getting worse.

She picked up the phone and dialed her folks' number in Pendleton one evening.

"Hello?" came Ben's deep, comforting voice.

"Hi, Daddy. How's Mom?"

"Fine, sweetie. How are all my little imps doin'?"

"We're fine," she replied. "Dad, I need to talk to you and Mom." A sadness in her voice told her dad that something in their lives had gone terribly wrong.

CHAPTER 6

THE SITUATION

Melissa Hathaway walked in first when they arrived together that afternoon in August. She had that determined gait and set look on her face, a lady in her thirties, with strong, angular features, possessing a simple beauty and graceful frame. She bore a sensitivity — especially in her eyes — that told me she had been touched to the core by something that she and Ron were experiencing together. I knew from having talked with her that her husband, Ron, faced a drunk driving conviction. He had some papers from the state of Oregon "about another matter — a child support obligation." Ron, with dark hair, slouched in the chair next to Melissa. She nodded to him to go first. Reaching across the desk, he flashed a tired, crooked smile and handed me the crumpled yellow and white drunk driving and diversion forms. He had taken time off from work. So had she. The drive from Springfield to Portland had taken almost three hours. He slowly took off his Caterpillar hat, laying it on the floor next to him. I noticed that the tips of his two ears tilted out from beneath his dark hair in a rather unusual, slightly triangular fashion.

Most couples coming in for the first time and sharing their distress hold hands. Ron and Melissa were no exception. I explained to Ron that a conviction for drunk driving could jeopardize his driver's license and in turn his job. I noticed the cords in his neck grow taut. Melissa's hand withdrew from his, tears slowly rolling from the corners of her deep brown eyes. Ron's job and their financial livelihood were in jeopardy unless Ron could obtain an occupational permit. We discussed briefly how he might qualify for the diversion program. The alcohol evaluation and counseling program would be very expensive. Melissa looked tensely at Ron the whole time.

Then Ron pulled the dirty white envelope and papers marked "State of Oregon" out of his torn jacket pocket and handed them over to me. The papers were worn and smeared in places. The grease-marked edges were soiled and crumpled. It was the mother's Affidavit of Paternity. This couple needed answers and answers quick. Fifteen years was a long time. Ron was the designated father. He had never even seen the child, Samuel Whitman.

I knew that the questions I must ask Ron would seem painfully embarrassing and out of place for Melissa to hear. "When did you meet Linda? How long did you know her socially? Did other men know her socially or sexually? How did you know her socially? Did you have sexual relations with Linda? How many times? When and where was the last time you remember having sexual relations with Linda? Was it during the period of conception? What were the circumstances? Did you ejaculate?"

The evasive answers Ron threw back reflected more his anger at the state and Linda than any real attempt to focus his recollection. Melissa's bewildered looks told me that Ron's defensiveness bothered her.

"Ron, did you use birth control? Did you wear a condom?" I asked.

"No," came the reply. "Why should I have?" he asked, with an almost amused look. "I was too damned drunk to remember anything." Melissa, shifting in her chair, stared out the window.

"Did Linda use birth control?" I asked.

"We all knew her from high school. She was always on the pill," he casually replied. Melissa continued to stare, her hands tensing, lips pressed tight. Ron quickly glanced at his wife.

"Will there be blood tests?" he nervously quizzed me.

"Yes," I replied.

"How soon?"

"As soon as the paperwork is completed and sent into the state contesting the paternity," I replied.

"What about the fee?" Ron and Melissa did not have money to pull out of any savings account. I looked over at Melissa, who nodded at me to get my attention.

"Well, my folks talked me into getting a part-time job so we can pay for this," she said rather forlornly. "But my pay at the medical clinic only nets about $400 to $500 a month, at best." She was looking directly at me. Her eyes had a vulnerable look, imploring me not to repeat the same script she'd heard so often before from other lawyers.

Melissa told me about having to leave her youngest, hyperactive son to fend for himself with his brother, while she worked days as a clerk/receptionist to pay for the mountain of legal expenses. She glanced at Ron. Ron avoided her look, seemingly unaware of the impact her working and his legal problems were having on Josh's world. On Ron's whole family.

Fifteen years — $26,000.00. A single mother with a fifteen-year-old boy named Samuel Whitman from a far off time.

Who was Linda? When did Linda go on public assistance? When Linda went on public assistance, did she know of Ron's whereabouts? Did she tell the state where he was? Why had the state waited fifteen years?

I knew that I could not possibly provide answers to all of their questions. But at least I could make reasonable attempts at the first few. The next day I contacted the support enforcement agency responsible for sending the letter.

"Hi, Doreen, what's cookin'?" Doreen Wilshire, the receptionist with the Support Enforcement Division, answered the phone and recognized my voice.

"Well, hello stranger. What are you bothering us for this time?" she chided.

"Oh, I need to talk to Jessie, Doreen. Another paternity case," I added. "Man's name is Ron Hathaway. The mother is Linda Aguilar, Case No. SED 177 ID 0347." I knew the routine well and so did Doreen. A plump lady in her fifties, she had worked at the agency for over ten years. She had taken so many phone calls from errant fathers and frantic single mothers, I wondered why she was still there. The men were always angry. The mothers were usually scared to death that the state was finally going to unite their children with long lost, strange men, their biological fathers.

"Hang on to your britches and I'll patch you through to Jessie," she chuckled again.

"Hey, guy, what's on the docket this week?" came Jessie Jacob's deep, resonant voice. An investigator for the support enforcement agency, he was a gentle giant of a man. I liked Jessie because he was unconventional and sported a backwoods beard and wore those bright red and green flannel shirts. And huge white suspenders. And I enjoyed the big man's earthy wit.

Jessie had been with the agency forever. He knew what I wanted and I knew the agency's scripted answers he would throw back at me. I knew he really didn't like the script that well, though. Punctuating the formalities of our conversation, Jessie's sense of humor always percolated. He'd joke about some agency screw-up or a person he had met who didn't fit the norm. For me, Jessie was a maverick whose wit was contagious, especially when I heard his chair squeak beneath his almost 300-pound weight.

"Well, Jessie, let's schedule some DNA tests for Hathaway and the other half of this family. Can we do this right away?" I asked.

"Certainly. Just make sure your man's available."

"No problem," I assured him. "Ya know, Jessie, it's been fifteen years since this kid was born. Ron didn't have a clue as to the young-ster's existence. Now I know what you are going to say before I even ask the question. But can you give me some inkling on Linda and the kid? All I have is a Notice and Finding of Financial Responsibility, an Affidavit of Paternity signed by the mother and a public assistance accounting of the state debt. And $26,000 staring my client in the face," I punctuated.

"Well, you know you're going to have to get a court order for those public assistance records."

"Oh, you're always making me chase down the Interstate to get those damn public assistance records," I laughed. "O.K., tell the legal staff I'll file a motion to compel production of Linda's public assistance records. Am I gonna need to compel production of her address and phone number, too?"

"You know the rules as well as I do, fella," Jessie chided me again. "You've got to pull teeth because those records are confidential." He and I both knew the game that had to be played.

"Well, O.K. Jessie, I'll go ahead and do my thing. But let's get these damned blood tests scheduled right away. My people are chomp-ing at the bit." I paused. "Now look what you've done to me. Just ruined my day," I continued. "Have to chase all the way down to the judge in Lane County for those records."

"Sure thing," the big man replied. I heard his chair squeak again and we both chuckled.

"Say hello to Georgia and the kids for me, Jessie, and take care," I closed. Already a grandfather, Jessie was almost a modern aberration: a happily married family man. He had fathered two daughters and had adopted his eldest daughter. He was not going to close our conversa-tion without updating me on his kids. He was especially proud of the basketball teams he and his wife now coached for his two teenage daughters. I listened to Jessie's play-by-play banter, picturing him running up and down the court, panting and hollering plays to the girls. I imagined his plump middle bouncing up and down in time with the dribble of the basketball, his deep-socketed eyes anxiously darting back and forth above his bushy beard, expecting plays to unfold as a result of his always gentle, patient coaching.

It took the rest of fall and into the first chilly month of winter to complete the DNA blood testing. Ron and Melissa called me from time to time to share their agonizing over what Melissa came to refer to as their "situation." Finally the results of the DNA tests arrived.

* * * * *

It was the week before Christmas when we next met. There were no bright, holiday faces or Christmas-wrapped packages. Talk of celebration did not accompany Ron or Melissa, only the awful presence of the paternity papers and their hope that the blood test would end the nightmare.

If Ron were not excluded, then they confronted a far more serious problem. The possibility of counseling was the only way I knew that Ron and Melissa might weather the storm. How they would pay for such counseling was beyond me. Ron's health insurance from Dahlberg Construction provided no coverage.

"Ron, the DNA test results did not exclude you as the father."

"What does that mean?" he blinked at me. Melissa, always seated next to Ron with an earnest look, stared at me, immobile.

"The test results indicate that the probability of paternity is 99.77%. This means that you cannot be excluded as the biological father. This percentage means that there is a very high probability based upon the DNA match testing that you could be the biological father." I knew that I did not need to go any further explaining the technical details of the genetic testing results. Ron and Melissa did not want to deal with scientific niceties now. They wanted the bottom line.

I thought the Xerox photos of Ron, Linda and Sam, which accompanied the test results, might provide further proof and help Ron reach acceptance in his own mind. I leaned across and placed the photocopies in front of Ron.

"Ron, maybe these photos will help provide some answers," I said, trying to sound reassuring. Linda's image was on top. There appeared a plump lady obviously in her forties, dowdy with a serious look, face slightly pockmarked with high cheekbones and a prominent, almost noble but slightly crooked nose. Her darkish hair was cut short. She stared out at Ron. Melissa leaned forward for a closer look. I slowly flipped to the next image — Sam. Melissa's look turned to astonishment as she glanced over at her husband. Ron's face turned very pale.

There was an unmistakable similarity. Dark hair. A broad, slightly crooked grin covered the boy's face. His nervous eyes were set below dark eyebrows, with the same cleft chin and jet black hair. A ring hung from the boy's left ear lobe. But the protruding ear tips were the dead giveaway. Melissa's expression of recognition did not amuse Ron.

"That kid doesn't look like me at all!"

I kept my counsel. My attempt to reach a reconciliation had not worked. Now Melissa sat in her chair, mute.

"Well Ron," I said. "It's your call."

"What the hell do I do now?" Ron shot back. "Tell me how I can get out of this mess, because I know I can," he stated defiantly. Melissa turned and stared at her husband. "Hell, a friend I used to work with told me how he got out of payin' support to his ex and the whole thing." Melissa rolled her eyes.

"Forget that crap," I told him. "I don't know what you've been told, but running away will only make matters worse. For starters, the feds and the states have ways of locating parents who owe support. Employers who don't cooperate with the law can get hammered. Employees, too. The child support enforcement system now is a lot more efficient then it used to be. Just like the IRS."

"Well that's damn comforting," exclaimed Ron, his voice frankly hostile, his face reddening. Melissa knew that I had unwittingly tread too close to her husband's danger zone. "What the hell do you suggest I do, then?" Ron was testy — emotionally unnerved.

"Well, the DNA test results mean that we have to prepare for trial, Ron. A trial could cost you about $1,500 to $2,500," I added. I wanted this couple to confront the financial question up front.

"Can I really get a fair paternity trial?" Ron asked. "What are the chances of them finding me guilty?" It was characteristic of men in Ron's position to equate fatherhood with guilt. I knew that financial concerns were the furthest thing from his mind. He needed to save face.

"Given the DNA tests, a jury would probably find you to be the biological father. All they need is testimony from Linda that she had sex with you and that you might have had conversations with her about the pregnancy."

"Shit, I never spoke to that woman about any pregnancy. God damn it, she's just a lying bitch on welfare!" Ron, his face now flushed crimson with anger, was out of his chair. "I want you to go to bat for me, for chrissakes!" Melissa had been staring out the window, her face very tense. She turned to me with an imploring look, her eyes riveted to mine.

"Ron, to get a fair trial, I'm going to need to go after the public assistance records. I need to see who Linda listed as the father of this child when she first applied for public assistance for the kid years ago. Then I can take Linda's deposition — her statement. I'll try and point out any inconsistencies between her public assistance records and her deposition testimony," I explained. "Finally, if you are found to be the father, I need to know whether you want visitation with the child. If so, we must bring Linda into this paternity case. The court will have to order the state to give me her address and phone number so that I can get her served with legal papers. Then we can settle all the issues of paternity and visitation and child support in one hearing. That is the only way you're going to get a fair trial."

Ron, still standing, looked totally confused.

"I don't know," he said, shaking his head.

"Ron, we do have a pretty good clue where Linda and Sam might be living," I said, trying to offer some reassurance. "The state files these paternity cases in the county where the mother or the child are living. Your case was filed in Eugene, the Lane County seat. That means Linda could be close at hand." Melissa looked uncomfortably at Ron. Ron, glancing down at the blue-carpeted floor, slowly sucked in air. I knew he and Melissa had no idea how Sam would fit into their lives. More importantly, Ron was confronted with a bigger decision.

"'Lissa, do you think I should call this Linda? Maybe I could talk some sense into her." Ron was being naive; Melissa wasn't amused.

"We can't really afford the expense of a $2,500 trial," she said firmly to me. "We can barely scrape by now. Even with my part-time job. Ron's diversion program has already gotten too expensive," she concluded fatalistically.

"I don't give a damn what it's going to cost," Ron burst out, standing now by the door. "All this slut has ever done is party, have kids and collect welfare. She lives off the public dole, God damn it! She would lie about anything."

"Oh Ron, will ya shut up!" Melissa angrily shot back. Her veins grew tense, her body erect in her chair, both hands clutching the armrests. She moved her stare from Ron directly towards me.

"Whoah, hold on a second, folks," I said, trying to soothe.

"Ah, shit. Screw it all anyway!" Ron said as he reached for the door knob.

"Come on now, let's get a grip. Calm down — time out!" I didn't want Ron to lose control. He stood motionless.

"Please, Ron. Will you just calm down and listen for a change," Melissa implored.

"Let me explain a few things to you. Sit down, Ron," I added, motioning with my hand towards his chair. Ron sat down. Now it was Melissa's turn, before I had my say.

"Ron's drinking has just gotten out of hand. We can't pay for all of these depositions for Linda and all of this legal stuff for a paternity case if we're simply going to lose. Ron drinks all the time. We just don't have the money." The firmness of Melissa's tone and her mention of his drinking made Ron bristle. Exhaling slowly, he finally returned to a slouched position in his chair.

"Can I continue to drive to work?" Ron asked, extending his hands as if pleading for the answers he wanted to hear.

"Not if you continue to screw it up and drink, Ron," I replied. "They'll bust you and nail your sorry ass to the jailhouse floor, and I guaran-damn-tee you your family's going to suffer," I said, staring directly at Ron. "You need to make sure you only drive during the times specified on your occupational permit." I hoped that my firmness would settle him down. Ron continued his disdainful slouch.

"O.K.," he muttered, glancing quickly at Melissa.

"Right off the bat, the first thing we need to do is to make sure that you stick to your diversion program and counseling. I will file a motion to compel production of Linda's public assistance records. We will see what we can find. After we get these records, I will let you know where we should go from there." I hoped that the answers I was giving might reassure Melissa somewhat. Her look of emptiness prompted me to move to the topic I thought uppermost in her mind.

"Ron, you screw up and get arrested for drunk driving again, and you will have a financial debt load that will put your ass through the pavement, I can assure you." Ron nodded at me knowingly. Oddly, he and I both started to grin at each other. I knew, instinctively, that my direct common sense might break through Ron's anger.

Ron and I finally were able to reconstruct some of the facts and circumstances of his meeting with Linda so long ago that night in Pendleton.

They had first mellowed out at a bar, followed by more drinking and dancing. Ron's recollection was cloudy, though, covered with blurred images which eventually found them in bed together — he wasn't really sure at whose place. Ron told me he had passed out. He vaguely remembered waking up, going home with friends, forgetting about Linda or that the drunken blowout had even occurred. He had left Pendleton then.

Privately I reached my conclusion. We simply would not prevail on the issue of paternity if we were going to try Ron's case in any orthodox fashion. He was faced with the DNA test results and the obvious physical resemblance to Sam. Still, I sensed that something had occurred here which was far more unsettling than the disappointing DNA results or even Ron and Melissa's situation.

CHAPTER 7

THE STATE'S SECRET

A mounting apprehension consumed me as I drove down to the Lane County courthouse in Eugene that brisk winter morning. The tops of the stands of Douglas and Grand Fir on either side of the freeway gently bowed and nodded, telegraphing the approach of a Willamette Valley January wind and rain storm. I arrived in the college town of Eugene, the county seat, just before the rain broke.

The Lane County Courthouse, a modern two story brick, steel and cement structure, was situated off one of downtown Eugene's main streets lined with leafless ornamental trees. The wide building with flat roof faced the street with a low-slung portico walkway. I walked up through the portico, past the carefully landscaped lawn and shrubbery, through the front glass doors, and up the stairway to the windowless courtroom.

The oak-paneled, arid courtroom of Judge Thomas Moriarty that morning seemed a sterile contrast from the black angus cows, the blowing leaves, and the billowing gray and white clouds of the Willamette Valley. The brightly lit courtroom was crammed with lawyers and their clients, awaiting criminal arraignment.

I looked around for Felicia Simmons, the assistant attorney general and head of the agency's paternity unit for western Oregon. I was surprised at being told she would be appearing for the state and opposing my motion to compel production of Linda's public assistance records. I finally spotted her seated next to the wall at the far end of the room, the furthest away from the jury box. A stack of files was piled on her lap. She was staring pensively ahead from behind thick-rimmed glasses. Impeccably groomed, Felicia's outer navy blue suit coat was completely buttoned, her pantsuit neatly pressed.

With a proper New England family upbringing, Felicia Simmons had grown up and attended school in Springfield, Massachusetts. A slender red-headed woman in her mid forties, she was the mother of twin daughters now in high school. She met her husband, Steve, at Harvard Law School and graduated in the top third of her class of '72. Steve, an Oregonian, had graduated from Harvard Law a year ahead of Felicia and took an associate position with a prestigious Portland law firm, handling the very sophisticated and expensive corporate legal work that silver stocking law firms handle. They settled in Oregon, she had once told me, because she liked the Cascades.

I liked Felicia. Possessing such compassion, as well as an astute legal mind, I wondered why she hadn't gone the way of so many of her other brilliant Harvard classmates including her husband, handling the lucrative corporate mergers, buyouts and spinoffs. She told me it was her "compassion for the downtrodden orphaned refugees" of an American family system which she saw as slowly disintegrating.

Felicia Simmons wielded her courtroom brilliance with telling force. Her finely honed analytical skills cut through an adversary's case like a rapier blade. Her closing arguments in paternity cases, especially the ones tried to a jury, were powerful, devastating.

The wait was boring. The shuffling of papers accompanied the annoying sound of lawyers constantly opening and snapping shut their briefcases, talking with clients and other lawyers. Folks entered and left the courtroom. Finally a tall, gangly fellow, the bailiff, strode into the courtroom through a door at the front, to the right of the judge's bench. He was followed by an attractive young woman in her late twenties — the court reporter — carrying a small machine with a keyboard. She seated herself next to the desk where the bailiff sat, in front of the judge's oak-paneled bench. I knew Judge Moriarty would be on the bench within a few short minutes. I walked over to where Felicia was seated.

"Hi, Felicia," I began. "I'm sure surprised to see you down here in Eugene this morning. Shouldn't you be in Salem handling more important stuff?" My kidding met with a broad smile.

"Hey, good to see you again. Yeah, just wanted to get away from the tedium of my office for a change," she replied. "Just waiting my turn here along with everyone else. Did you enjoy the drive down?" she added very politely.

"Yeah, I like to get out of the office and see the valley."

"Me, too. The driving gives me a chance to think over my important cases." Her statement worried me. With a busy trial schedule, why was Felicia Simmons in Eugene this particular morning? Was my case one of her "important cases?" I knew her simple, genuine qualities hid a sharp instinct for the jugular. I worried about what damage she would do to my motion to compel those records.

"Do you have our case?" I asked, trying to appear nonchalant. "Ron Hathaway. The mother is Linda Aguilar." I glanced at the mountainous stack of manila folders on her lap, perhaps thirty case files in all. "Where are we on your huge list of cases, Felicia?" We both laughed, knowing that her work load that morning was far heavier than mine. She fumbled through the stack and found Ron's file.

"You're seventh on my list." She glanced up at me through clear thick-rimmed glasses with a freckled smile, the lenses magnifying her light blue eyes to almost twice their normal size.

"Can you push me to the top so I can get the heck out of here and back up to Portland within a week?" I asked, chuckling and nodding to her.

"Sure, no problem." She carefully pulled the file out and placed it on top.

"Thanks, Felicia. Hope these damn criminal arraignments don't take all morning." I was getting restless. Felicia went back to being pensive and stoic.

As I walked to the back of the courtroom, everyone stood. A hush fell over the room. I instinctively turned around. In walked Judge Moriarty with a long stride and determined look. He plunked all five-feet-five inches of his portly frame behind the bench. He placed his bifocals on his nose and promptly nodded to the clerk to hand him the morning's list of criminal arraignments. As he took the stack of files from the clerk, I noticed his dark hairy arms protruding from the front of his black robe.

A clean-shaven man in his fifties, Judge Moriarty had worked the first few years of his career in private practice. He then had spent fifteen years with the district attorney's office in Lane County before being appointed to the bench by the governor. Thinking about his background caused me to worry. Would he favor the state? I wondered.

I was hoping to get all of Linda's public assistance records as well as her present address and phone number. I knew I would get Sam's birth certificate and hospital birth records. I would also get background information on Linda: where she had lived, the people in her household, her marriages, any divorces, and her health history. But her present address would be necessary so I could serve her with the legal papers. That way I could involve her in the paternity proceedings so that Ron could get a complete and fair trial. He might want visitation rights with Sam should he be found to be the biological father. But then, again, maybe not.

The really crucial records I needed would be difficult to pry loose from the state. Felicia would put up a fight. These assistance records would tell me where she lived and who Linda listed as the father fifteen years ago when she applied for public assistance. The law required mothers receiving assistance for a child born out of wedlock to name the man who had fathered the child. I wondered what those records would show. Did she name Ron or some other man as Sam's father? I wasn't at all sure how Judge Moriarty would rule. The criminal arraignments dragged on and on.

"State of Oregon ex rel Adult and Family Services Division versus Ron Hathaway." I heard Judge Moriarty say the name "Hathaway" and I was on my feet approaching counsel table. Felicia Simmons was already seated at counsel table to my left. The judge's high-backed cushioned leather chair squeaked. I almost burst out laughing as I approached. It had suddenly dawned on me that Judge Moriarty was really a shorter, portlier version of Jessie Jacobs. But the amusing thought immediately evaporated as I sat down at the long glossy-topped, mahogany counsel table, five feet away from Felicia. Would I get those records and would we be able to locate Linda? The room was silent. The judge glared at me.

"Counsel, this is your motion to compel," Judge Moriarty stated firmly, his eyes riveted to mine through the top of his bifocals. Head cocked sideways, he braced his chin and left cheek against his left hand, his silver pen pointing menacingly into the air from his clenched right fist. "I read your motion and accompanying memorandum of points and authorities. Do you have anything to add?" His bearing was very direct, his tone somewhat sarcastic. He looked serious. And annoyed. His question almost seemed to be an admonition not to add anything. He had waded through a mountain of cases during that morning's criminal docket and was anxious to get through the civil cases in the short time remaining before noon recess.

"Good morning, Your Honor." I knew I needed to keep my presentation short. "Nothing other than the fact that the state has waited fifteen years to bring this paternity case. We need to see what those early public assistance records disclose. We need to know who Linda Aguilar listed as the father of the little boy, Your Honor. Secondly, I cannot bring this mother into this paternity action unless I know her present whereabouts — her address, her phone number. That's all I have, Your Honor." I sat down and glanced over at Felicia. The judge leaned forward, pressing his lips together, staring at Ms. Simmons from the top of his glasses.

"Ms. Simmons? Anything you want to add?"

"Well, as you know, it is the state's position that these welfare records and the address of the obligee-mother — the grant recipient — are confidential. This confidentiality is protected by federal and state regulations. In addition, I don't think any of the information is going to be relevant to the issue of paternity."

I jumped on my feet. "Your Honor, I — ." Judge Moriarty, putting his left hand up, waved me off in mid sentence. I sank down, my stomach now a tense knot. He's made up his mind. Felicia has done it again. He's gonna rule against us! I was frozen in mid thought when the judge spoke.

"I am ordering that the state produce all requested birth and medical information on the youngster, the mother's health and marital history, and any information regarding Mr. Hathaway's contacts with her and the boy." He paused, thinking of his next move. I held my breath. "The state will also produce for inspection only those public assistance records filled out by the mother having to do with who she thought the father of this youngster was, and any information she might have given the state about the members of her household or about the putative father's whereabouts." The judge had given us a partial victory. He had at least conceded that the paternity information Linda had given to the state fifteen years ago might be relevant to this case. I waited for the judge to finish. What about Linda's address?

"Finally," added Judge Moriarty, "I'm going to require the state to furnish the address and phone number of the mother's present whereabouts to Mr. Hathaway's counsel." The confidentiality wall had been broken.

"The purpose of this order is so that counsel may bring the mother into these paternity proceedings. We're going to have a full and complete adjudication of everyone's rights and obligations in one, single proceeding. That will be the Court's ruling." Motioning to me, the judge concluded, "Mr. Hathaway's counsel will prepare the order."

I nodded at Felicia, saying "Thank you, Your Honor."

The trip back to Portland on the Interstate snaked through a checkerboard of fields lined with distant, ridged woodlands. Farmhouses and sheep and cattle dotted the landscape. The winds breathed a crispness and freshness into the valley — more pleasant with the sun out than earlier that morning. What surprises will those records reveal to us? I wondered. Will Ron want to contact Linda? That question weighed heaviest on my mind. Maybe that's why the trip back to Portland, although more relaxing, seemed longer than the morning's journey to Eugene.

* * * * *

"The public assistance records tell us that Linda had applied for welfare fifteen years ago when she was pregnant with Sam," I informed the Hathaways. "Ron, she named you as the father right away. She listed your address at your folks business place in Pendleton." Ron stared at me with disbelief.

"Jesus Christ, those sons-a-bitches knew where I was the whole time!" he shot back. "Everyone knew Hathaway's Hardware. My parents have always known where I lived. Why did this happen?" The intense thrust of Ron's anger suffocated any legal answers I might have summoned.

"Ron, I can't tell you why it happened," I half-stammered, genuinely feeling at a loss. Then I began to relate to Ron and Melissa a sadder tale. It was a story of an Indian woman, now in her forties and nearly abandoned. She had lived a hard life.

Both of Linda's parents were dead. She had held down a few menial jobs waitressing and bartending in Pendleton and had been married twice, the last time to a man named Aguilar. When the child support payments stopped, the public assistance system would "kick in" and rescue her and her children. Linda had had five children, mostly by different men. She had been on public assistance intermittently since leaving high school. Her youngest daughter, Susan, had been on welfare for some time. Susan and her new baby were living with Linda and Linda's youngest child, a boy.

The father of Linda's youngest child, Tony Aguilar, was now paying some child support. This meant that Linda might be going off "the dole" sometime in the near future.

Linda's support group was largely nonexistent except for a few close friends. I knew their names. They were listed as witnesses on her behalf. They would testify at the paternity trial. Having been close to Linda when Ron passed through her life, they would be able to say things in court that would be revealing about Ron's actions and statements.

After reading the pubic assistance records and listening to Jessie Jacobs fill in sketchy details between basketball stories, more pieces of Linda and her son had slowly trickled out.

"Do you remember much about her folks?" I asked Ron.

"Nah, just that she pretty much raised herself. Remember her old man — Joe — really into rodeoing. Flipped off the back end of a bull one time at the roundup. Broke some ribs. One tough cookie." Ron paused. "Linda ran with a different crowd. Drank a lot. Got pregnant and had to leave high school her junior year, I guess."

"Well," I said, "there are a few surprises." Ron leaned forward in his chair, listening intently. "She has a criminal history of welfare fraud and petty theft."

"What did I tell you about her, huh," retorted Ron, nodding at Melissa. "We can use this against her, can't we?" he asked enthusiastically.

"Possibly," I replied. I knew I could use this at the time of trial to attack her truthfulness. Unlike Ron, the prospect didn't excite me. "One of Linda's children was killed in a motor vehicle accident," I continued.

"What happened?" asked Melissa.

"Don't really know." I paused, watching Melissa's slow glance at Ron. "She also pled guilty to involuntary manslaughter — something about a shooting. She received a light jail sentence and parole." The two people before me were now totally mute, eyes transfixed to mine. There were things they couldn't comprehend and I wasn't equipped to help them.

Still, Linda was a mother who seemed different from all the others I'd seen. I learned that after years of instability, she was finally trying to settle down and raise her youngest child. She had somehow managed to escape her hard past in Pendleton. Evidently the few jobs she held had enabled her to move to Eugene with Sam, her daughter and her youngest boy. I knew it must have been difficult for this Indian woman.

I held back from Ron, not wanting to mention that I was not completely clear about Linda's health history. The sketchy information I had seemed to indicate that years of drinking and hard living might have taken their toll.

"What about the boy, Samuel?" Melissa finally asked. "Do you know anything about him?"

I looked back at her tense expression, thinking how difficult it would be for them to comprehend. Jessie had told me of his sense of loss about Sam, raised by a single mother on welfare most of his life, and how this youngster had grown apart from everyone.

"I guess the boy had a tough time in school over in Pendleton," I replied. "Sam's been in a lot of trouble — arrests for drugs, alcohol abuse, petty theft."

"What the hell," retorted Ron, arms outstretched, now, as if imploring Melissa for help. "We can't deal with this," he continued, facing his wife. "How old is he, for chrissakes?"

"Fifteen, almost sixteen," I replied.

"Jesus H. Christ!" Ron exploded. "We can't raise this kid. I don't want him near Rob or Josh."

"Take it easy, Ron," I said, motioning with my hand for him to stay seated. Melissa had avoided looking directly at her husband. With a beaten expression, she was now staring out the window.

I told Ron and Melissa that I would contact Jessie and clarify whether or not Sam lived at home. I also needed more information about this woman's health. But I was now confronted with something even more troublesome.

"Ron, I have obtained the address and telephone number of Linda. Like I told you, she lives in Lane County now. We are going to file a motion to make her a party to these paternity proceedings. Then if you are found to be the father, we might be able to establish some kind of visitation."

"Jesus Christ Almighty!" Ron threw his hands into the air from his usual slouched position. His face reddening, he rose to an upright position in his chair, eyes fixed on Melissa. "Hon, Sam doesn't even have my last name. I don't even know who this kid is. How the hell am I going to have visits with him?"

"Ron, you're going to have to figure this one out for yourself," Melissa said evenly. I was surprised at her coolness, her detachment. Ron now returned a painful look my way.

"What should I do? Should I call this Linda and talk to her?"

I knew that these questions foretold that Ron was, after all, a star in a triangle consisting of a family which had been broken from its inception fifteen years ago. Yet, I wondered. How would Ron's entry at this late stage strike Linda and the child?

"Ron, I am a father with children of my own. I can tell you that the moral thing to do would be to call Linda and discuss this with her and find out about Sam," I said self assuredly. "However, from a strictly legal standpoint, I must advise you not to call Linda because anything you might say to her could be used against you at a paternity trial. You don't want to make any admissions that you're the father or say anything that would hurt you at the time of trial. She could repeat anything you say to her in any phone conversation with her." At this, Ron's jaw slackened, leaving his mouth hanging open.

"Honey, let's talk about this later," Ron finally muttered, as he pushed himself up out of his chair to leave. Melissa stared intently at her husband with glistening eyes. She got up slowly from her chair.

"Ron, I will do what I can to convince the state's attorney not to take this case to trial," I said, trying not to sound half-hearted, as Ron's back disappeared out the door. Melissa turned to me. Her deep, hazel brown eyes told the whole story of her aching.

"This is just tearing us apart," she said with such melancholy that I held my hand out to hers. Tears moistened the edges of her deep hazel eyes. "I want to do what's right, but I dunno if I can keep on," she sobbed quietly.

"Please try to keep him off the booze," I quietly told Melissa. "I'll be in touch." I held her right hand, now, with both of mine. "Try not to worry. I'll do my best, Melissa." She turned and followed her husband down the long hall to the elevator.

CHAPTER 8

THE MUMBLES CASE

The virtue of getting no business mail deliveries on weekends is that after the letter bombs are opened on Friday, you can enjoy at least a partial rest from the vicious paper wars till Monday. The letter arrived from the State Attorney's Office late that snowy Monday afternoon in February after I'd had so many conversations with Felicia Simmons and the folks at the state about Ron's case. I glanced at the unopenèd letter from the state of Oregon. It was perched on top of the usually thick stack of mail I found on my desk on Mondays. I stared at the thin, white envelope. My thoughts wove back to the last conversation I'd had with Felicia. I remembered feeling somewhat pessimistic and cynical afterwards.

"Hi, Doreen. Patch me through to Felicia, will ya?"

"Sure thing, sweetie," replied Doreen in her usual velvety-smooth voice. To others, her voice might seem distant and unsympathetic. But I knew Doreen. I admired her capacity to answer so many phone calls, to remember so many people's names through their voices. She had an amazing ability to calm very angry people. Men especially would call in, mad as hell. They'd holler and cuss at her about their child support. Maybe, sometimes, she would have a bad day.

"Hi, Felicia. I want to talk about this Hathaway case with you. Got a second?" I pictured Felicia, seated again, with that stack of files placed neatly on her desk in front of her, her thick-rimmed glasses perched on her nose. Her chair did not squeak when she talked to me. Her mind, as always, was well tuned.

"Hey fella. Are you going to make me drive down the Interstate again to try this case?" she asked warmly. "Or do you have a settlement offer I can't refuse?"

I was curt. "Felicia, I want you to listen to me for a minute."

"Sure, no problem," she said. It was a pet phrase. She was always so damned patient and polite before shooting holes in my cases. I was in for a tough sparring match, a thought which reminded me of the times I listened intently, as a child, to the world heavyweight boxing matches on the radio, my father seated next to me, the announcer graphically describing the battle between the titans. Now I realized that in an entirely different arena Ms. Simmons might outbox me and leave me completely devoid of any legal defenses for Ron Hathaway.

"Ron's case is really all about simple notions of fairness and justice," I started. "Fifteen years is no small amount of time. Felicia, you wrote second high paper in your constitutional law class. You know better than anyone that the phrase 'due process' is not a collection of stale words etched into some ancient document called the Bill of Rights." The bell had rung. The opening round had just begun.

"Hey, yeah, but what about Linda's due process rights, not just Ron's?" she threw back at me. I wasn't prepared for this. I reeled back, but not for long.

I waded in. "Wait a minute, now" I said. "'Due process' is a concept as alive as flesh and blood — the right of all citizens, no matter how despicable, to have some kind of notice." I was confident. I was ready to take on anybody. I was dancing like a butterfly. "Felicia, you know as well as I do that these men are entitled to some kind of formal notice from the state when the state takes upon itself the responsibility of putting 'bread' on the table for a youngster." I was puffed, proud of my constitutional agility.

"Counsel," Felicia said simply, "do you know what Linda has told us? After she knew she was pregnant with Sam, she talked to Ron about it. Didn't you know that? He already had 'notice' in my book." For an awful instant, I was hit with the intense, suffocating pain Max Schmeling must have felt when Joe Louis buried his gloved fist into the German's stomach at the end of the 1938 world heavyweight championship. A few seconds into the first round and Felicia Simmons already had me down for almost the full count. My beautiful pre-fight strategy, dancing like a butterfly, was clobbered with an iron fist composed of one brutal fact. And what had Ron actually remembered? After all, the misty cloud of booze had hung heavy over his story. "Well, counsel?" Felicia had been waiting patiently for me to gather my thoughts. I got up slowly from the mat.

"Felicia, it doesn't matter if Linda told Ron she was pregnant." I admit I was tentative, but I was swinging. "The fact of the matter is that she never told Ron he would owe the state $26,000. Felicia, you know we have state action here. Linda received public assistance." I paused, starting to get my wind back. "Are you telling me that some kind of private notice from Linda to Ron is actually going to satisfy the formality of giving that man proper notice that he would someday owe all this money to the state of Oregon?"

"Hey, he should have thought about that when he had sex with her, for God's sakes." The thought struck me as slightly absurd. Was Felicia really going to use this argument in court?

"Are you telling me that Ron, or any other man for that matter, receives notice of an accruing state debt every time he has sex with a woman? Come on, Felicia, really! That's an interesting argument concocted in fantasy land." I felt I had recovered and had just landed a pretty good shot.

"Well, counselor, I simply think that her telling Ron she was pregnant is good enough notice, constitutionally." She seemed to be fumbling, but I knew better. I wondered what Ron had forgotten or simply hadn't told me. I probed further.

"Hold on now, Felicia," I said, trying not to sound too cocky. "Ron's a hard working fella with a family and a lot of bills. You hand him a bill for $26,000 right out of the blue with no warning. Bam!" I exclaimed for emphasis.

"He should have thought of that when he slept with her," she shot back again.

"Oh, for crying out loud!" I was getting impatient. "Here we have a guy who has absolutely no inkling that the state is putting financial 'bread' on the table for this out-of-wedlock child, Sam. No idea. The state debt you say he owes keeps getting bigger and bigger each month, each year." I paused, expecting a response. Hearing none, I continued. "Yet you folks don't even bother to notify him? Don't even tell him that he might just have a support obligation that keeps getting bigger and bigger? Then you hand him and his family a bill for $26,000 at the end of fifteen years and tell him to 'have a nice day'?"

"Oh come on, now!" I could feel Felicia Simmons bridle with indignation at the other end.

"What do you expect the poor bastard to do?" I protested.

"Most of these deadbeats are going to cut and run anyway," she replied sarcastically.

"Of course they are," I added. "What do you expect them to do? The system has set itself up to fail — miserably, I might add." There, I had just about said it all.

"Well," she said, "you know the system isn't perfect." I had expected a better answer.

"Really? What a cop out. Snafu or no snafu, bureaucratic mess or not, do you think this is fair?" Silence from the other end. "I don't think you're gonna get the $26,000 under any circumstances, Felicia. Court's just not gonna make Ron pay. No notice, no due process. Period."

"We'll see," she stated flatly. "He got notice of these paternity proceedings. That's certainly sufficient in my book."

I wanted to prod further. "Can you tell me this — why didn't the state notify Ron that he might have an accruing state debt against him fifteen lousy years ago? Felicia, the records tell us that they knew where he was fifteen years ago, for crying out loud! Why wasn't the damned paternity action brought way back then?" I absolutely knew I now had her up against the ropes with this argument. Caught up in the heat of the battle, I wasn't expecting, nor was I ready for what the master was about to throw at me during the next round.

"You may be right, but you are overlooking several important points," she announced.

"Oh, really?" I asked with mock surprise.

"Well, can you tell me this?" she began somewhat sarcastically, mimicking my earlier question to her. "Do you have any idea what our budget constraints have been over the past fifteen years?"

"No."

"What about staff shortages?" she asked. "You know lack of staff can lead to snafus?"

"Yes, of course," I agreed. I felt she was laying a trap for me but wasn't sure when or where she was going to clobber me with the gloved fist of her logic.

"And of course I know you're aware that ten or fifteen, or even five years ago, the feds did not pressure the states to establish paternity like they do now."

"Sure, Felicia. But so what," I added, feeling I was being lured into a trap.

"Well, this sort of thing happens in other paternity cases as well. The sheer, overwhelming number of out-of-wedlock births has placed a terrible burden on our agency. Do you have any idea what our case-load has been the past several years? How many welfare paternity cases we process?"

"Oh, let's see. Hundreds," I threw back, confident that my number would tell her that I did not lack an appreciation of her agency's administrative and fiscal problems. But I had, once again, unknowingly stepped into her trap.

"Hundreds? Come on, get real. Try thousands," she asserted. "And, of those, hundreds and hundreds of these fathers just disappear." My neatly crafted notice argument suddenly seemed puny compared to the avalanche of reality she was unleashing on me. I knew that a 'due process' argument might not survive such an onslaught. "We couldn't even begin to hire the investigators we need to locate these deadbeats ten or fifteen years ago. You, of all people, should know that," she added. "This is a sound policy decision the agency has always made," she concluded. I was rankled by the way she seemed to sweep aside a solemn constitutional right to notice using so-called "agency policy." I had confronted this tactic before and it had always seemed so damned arrogant to me.

"Hang on a second, Felicia. What about the minimum rule of decency and fairness? When you have state action on behalf of a parent of a child born out of wedlock, isn't it just simple fairness to give timely notification to a person the mother designates as the father. Especially if she knows his whereabouts?" I knew I was coming back strong. Hearing no retort from Felicia and feeling confident, I impulsively thought of setting a trap for her. I moved in with my next question.

"Isn't it true that the state notifies married fathers every time their spouses or ex spouses have to go on public assistance?" I was proud of how deftly I was setting my trap.

"Yes, of course," came Felicia's reply. Excited at the prospect that I was about to deliver a telling shot, I now had a nearly fatal mental lapse. Never, ever violate the time-honored admonition for trial lawyers conducting cross-examination. Never, ever ask your opponent the question "Why?"

"Then why does the state have to treat Ron and other men like him any different?" I asked. "And the children, too," I threw in. "What's the percentage in doing that?" I felt confident that I finally had delivered one of my strongest legal combinations.

Felicia was quick to pounce. "What is a notice sent from the state going to do for men like Ron?" she asked. "All they're going to do is run. Statistics show that. That's why we only notify the married fathers. That's our policy. We can find them a hell of a lot easier." Once again, I felt chagrined. I hadn't done any damage.

"C'mon, Felicia. The purpose of a notice to Ron would have allowed him to at least provide for the needs of Sam a lot sooner by paying child support. It certainly would have reduced the terrible arrearage that was built up over the years. You people just simply wait too damn long to bring these paternity cases." I had uttered the words "you people," with special purpose for Felicia Simmons. A common phrase used by proper New England old-timers when referring contemptuously to those whose behavior they disapproved, I knew the words would rankle Felicia.

"There you go again, fella, belittling what we do. You guys never understand that these deadbeats won't pay child support unless and until they're pulled in by the pocketbooks. The taxpayers pay too damn much money simply because these jerks won't pay child support." I knew she had a good point. I also knew I needed a good comeback if Felicia Simmons was really going to take my arguments seriously. Better move in close and fast, now, or risk losing this match.

"Felicia, it doesn't take a rocket scientist to know that early on and consistent payment of support provides a bond between noncustodial parents and their children. Early notice from the state would provide an opportunity for at least some of these men you call deadbeats to prove themselves as fathers. You can't deny that earlier payment of support and the building of a bond is in the child's best interest." There, I had said it the best way I knew how. "Hell, you know there are plenty of studies demonstrating this fact of life," I added. I felt that I had finally obtained the upper hand. But, alas, I couldn't have been more naive.

"Yeah, and what about the lost opportunities which countless out-of-wedlock children face by not having real fathers in their lives. Most of these men are deadbeats and simply run away from their responsibilities." I felt as if she were swarming all over me again, using an all-too-familiar punch. What does losing a father really mean for kids? I wondered.

Felicia Simmons was right. Thousands ran away. Did it really make any difference whether Ron had private notice from Linda or more formalized notice from the state? If most of these men ran away, what was the point?

"Well, you people bring these paternity actions only when and if you're damned good and ready," I shot back. "That's the height of stupidity. The state can achieve a hell of a lot more by notifying these men sooner. The state is bound to collect more child support from those fathers who wish to settle the score by paying their support a lot sooner. Isn't that in the child's best interest?" I hoped that this appeal would leave an impression.

"Well, you might have a point there," she conceded. "But, you know, I still think Ron got notice when Linda told him she was pregnant with his child." This statement, again, left me annoyed. I wondered if Ron had really been truthful with me.

"Well, let's assume that you're correct, Felicia. Why, then, does the state need to treat married fathers any differently than fathers of children born out of wedlock? You're telling me that the state will send a formal notice to married fathers while they choose not to send a formalized notice to fathers of children born out of wedlock. This seems to be discriminatory, don't you think? If Ron is Sam's biological father, how is he any damned different than a married father?" I paused, expecting to hear an answer. "Doesn't Sam deserve just as much from the state as a kid who's father happens to be married to his mom?" I hoped that Felicia would now realize that the system had somehow utterly failed to assist Ron and other errant fathers to unite with children like Sam.

"Well, let me get back to you on this," she said. "I need to specially staff this case for review," she added. Her last remark offered some hope that our polite but intense telephone sparring match had not been totally disastrous for me. Still, I was pessimistic. Her arguments had bloodied me. Perhaps I had done the same to her.

Hanging up the phone, I remembered, now, how I had reacted to the sum and substance of Felicia's last shot.

"Ah, but the state knows best." The thought struck me then, as it did now, as comically ironic.

"The ultimate 'mumblefuck' case," I added to myself, laughing out loud. In law school we had joked that it would be an honor to someday handle the ultimate and oft-quoted "mumbles" case. The "mumbles" case was the one with all of the classic screw-ups in it, the case where the state seemingly had all of the policy answers yet none of the solutions. I smiled. Ron's situation was, indeed, such a case.

A decision had to be made. My eyes were glued to the still unopened envelope from the State Attorney's Office lying in front of me. I reminded myself now, on this chilly Monday afternoon, that I'd finally have to deal with Ron and Melissa Hathaway's painful situation.

Seeking temporary refuge, I glanced out my window at what had become my favorite pastime — the landmark wall-fountain beneath the State Office Building. On hot July days, children would dash about in the broad expanse of the pool, splashing and dodging the arching, narrow spigot and gargoyle streams, climbing over the labyrinth of cement steps and ledges on either side of the main fixture. A sharply pitched cantilevered rock and cement trough jutted from the wall. It bisected the fountain, sending cold water cascading down, crashing over those youngsters lucky enough to crowd directly underneath.

On this particular February afternoon, the fountain was peaceful, deserted. Icicles hung as decorations from the foot ledges and the end of the jutting trough. A slick shine coated the interior of the jutting shute, a reminder that the Willamette Valley was now icy cold beneath the stillness. The pond was covered with a hardened freeze, empty save for leafy debris and white pigeon droppings.

I would go there, now, with the state attorney's letter, sit and count the icicles.

CHAPTER 9

LITTLE PAWLIK'S SECRET

Almost a year earlier, the old weather-beaten 1970 brownish gray Oldsmobile, chrome rear fender crumbling, had pulled up to the corner of Seventh and Willamette Street in Eugene. The incessant Oregon rainstorm that April afternoon had soaked everything. A gray black cloud billow hung over the town, giving the air a gloomy pall. The creaking Olds made a slow, wide turn into the puddle strewn parking lot alongside the recently renovated, nondescript three story wooden structure.

Behind the wheel, her head straining to find a parking space, sat Linda Pawlik Whitman. Her long, black hair was loosely fixed behind her head in a barrette, several strands pasted down her right ear from having been in the wind and rain. She squinted between the wiper blades, accentuating her high russet cheek bones. Her prominent nose was slightly crooked along the top ridge. She wore an old, loose-fitting dark leather jacket, frayed at the edges. A bright blue, green, orange and red string of beads hung around her neck and down across a white shirt covering her flaccid breasts. Her large torso was restrained with a single lap belt, her stomach protruding, hanging over the top of the belt. Her loosely fitting dark slacks were a mismatch with her tight fitting white shirt. The only color match was her tennis shoes, beige, now rain soaked and soiled.

Her foot first pressed the gas, then abruptly hit the brake pedal. The female occupant in the passenger seat next to her was suddenly thrown forward, barely catching herself on the dash with both arms outstretched.

"Whoa, Linda, watch what you're doing!" exclaimed Doris Wallport from the front seat. "Almost took my teeth out," she added, glancing around.

"Geez, can't you learn how to drive?" came the fifteen-year-old boy's sullen remark from the back seat. Samuel Little Pawlik Whitman, formerly reclining in the back seat, now had to put up with the indignity of waking to the jarring motion and having to exert himself to a full sitting position.

"Shut up, Pawlik," retorted his mother. She, too, could dish it out, knowing that the older the kid got the more he really disliked her mimicking his given Indian nickname "Little Pawlik." "Get ready and straighten yourself out. We're goin' in and talk to the investigator and I want you to pay attention," she added. "And don't fall asleep on me in there, you unnerstan'?"

"Lay off will ya," her son retorted contemptuously. "Bitch," he half muttered to himself. For a fleeting instant the youngster had an urge but caught himself. He dared not utter that foulest of epithets, no matter what his mother said or did — the word "squaw."

Linda turned and glowered at her son, but made no reply.

"Doris, you bring that list of questions we went over?" she asked her friend. Doris Wallport checked the front pocket of her white coat, feeling the slip of white paper and nodded.

"Sure thing, hon, I've got it right here." A slightly older version of Linda, Doris Wallport had been Linda's best friend ever since the days in Pendleton. A plumpish Anglo in her mid forties, Doris was a mother earth type of woman. Like Linda, she had lived a hard life herself.

Doris Wallport's constant pride was how she had been able to "transition" herself off the public assistance "dole" and into a self-sufficient existence. An intelligent woman, she had graduated from high school in Pendleton but had been trapped in an abusive marriage with her two daughters, now grown. Following her divorce, she had been forced onto public assistance, her ex-husband rarely, if ever, paying support or seeing his daughters. With some help from her social worker, Doris went back to school, taking evening community college classes and learning bookkeeping and computer skills. She, too, had left Pendleton, but a year ahead of Linda, coming out to Eugene and taking a job as a food stamp intake clerk. The college town atmosphere appealed to her because she had always loved to read; mostly mysteries but local history and Indian lore had lately become her fascination.

Doris was more than Linda's best friend, really. More a kindred sister. They had both been through a lot together since childhood, a strong rope which bound them together. Linda had shown Doris how possible it was to survive being a part of two cultures, yet not really being a part of either one.

But Doris' friendship with Linda had endured mostly because she had learned to tread lightly when Linda confided about the things she felt most vulnerable. She was Linda's guiding light in Linda's own transition to Eugene and now in the trial that Linda was about to undergo.

Linda wheeled her beaten Oldsmobile into a parking space, nudging the front end of the rusty chrome bumper up above a cement barrier with a sickening, grinding sound. Linda slowly backed off, bringing the car to a rest and turning the engine off.

"Jesus, I should've driven you two women here," snapped Sam sarcastically. Linda whirled around. Sam, wearing his long black hair underneath a reversed baseball cap, below which dangled a silver earring from a punctured left ear lobe, glared at his mother with a crooked grin.

"Come on, Sam, tuck yourself in and look intelligent for once. This is serious business." Sam had fallen asleep, letting his loosely fitting, multi-colored flannel shirt unbutton, revealing his favorite psychedelic purple and gold heavy metal T-shirt. Beltless, his coal black baggy pants were askew. "The kid looks like he's just been to a rock concert," remarked his mother to Doris.

"Didn't really want to be here anyway, dammit!" Sam exclaimed. "Already had things planned. Wanted to hang out with Tom today," he mumbled insolently.

"Tom Strickler is nobody I want you associatin' with when you're s'posed to be at school," his mother lectured. "You didn't skip school again, did you — dammit?"

Sam looked at his mother, saying nothing.

Never a good student, Sam had had problems in Pendleton. The move to Eugene hadn't helped either. Having been held back a year, Linda knew her ninth grader didn't have the drive. "I don't want you hangin' around that doper," Linda added, emphasizing her disgust.

"Get off my back, will ya?" he yelled back. Sam glared at his mother. "This ain't easy for me, neither!"

* * * * *

Indeed, from the very beginning, things had not been easy. Samuel Little Pawlik Whitman had not come into the world head first, but by breech through Caesarean section, leaving his mother not only with an abdominal scar, but a scar inside from the difficulties she'd faced with her pregnancy.

Without adequate prenatal care, Linda had trudged into the public clinic in downtown Pendleton twice a month with her two daughters in tow for checkups, her meager public assistance grant not entitling her to ultrasound or other diagnostic tests. The baby had never taken to breast feeding like her two older daughters did.

She nicknamed him "Little Pawlik." Not so much out of a bond with the baby, but more because of the way the child had grown inside of her, always "pawing" at her insides, and causing a different kind of back discomfort which, unlike her first two pregnancies, never seemed to go away. Perhaps it was the incessant discomfort that led her to the realization that this child should have part of her name as well. She cared for him, but not like other mothers of first-borns did — out of a sense of love and compassion. Her caring was more out of a reluctant sense of duty, as she was more caught up with the attention focused upon her by the man who became her first husband, Salvador Rodriguez.

Little Pawlik's first memories were not of his mother, but of being left alone for long periods. He remembered looking up at a ceiling forever and crying, wailing through a succession of nights and days while, every now and then, his two sisters would come into the room from their play. He would see their faces. They would pick him up and hold him gently for awhile then rock him back to sleep.

His first recognition of his mother was of her face, big and round, with her high cheek bones and jet black hair and deep dark eyes. He loved her eyes, was transfixed by them, never really noticing her inability to smile very often. Her mouth, for the most part, was slack and inert. In those early years, Little Pawlik never saw his mother or Salvador Rodriguez together.

Little Pawlik's earliest pleasant memories were those of his two older sisters, Patricia Whitecloud and Susan. Pat, a decade older than he was, became his surrogate mother, diapering him, feeding him and watching out after him when Linda was gone. Susan, more of an older sister, played with her younger brother.

The child remembered, though, that when Salvador — his mother called him Sal — was around, music at their place would get louder, there would be more adults and more shouting. And fights would break out — terrible fights.

Sal was a brute of a man — boorish and burly — with gaudy blood-red tattoos on his huge, hairy arms, biceps and shoulders. Sal was a drinker, too. He became surly and morose when drunk. Sal's body emitted a constant sour odor of stale beer and whiskey, mixed with sweat. His breath spread forth in rancid waves from large, puffy lips. His eyebrows loomed as dark clouds over even darker eyes, all set in an immense head covered with black curly hair. His boulder-like shoulders dripped with shiny sweat. A massive chest, covered with bristly black hair, swelled into a globular beer belly, though it looked as hard as iron. A short, stout neck rose above a rounded back. His face, his body, reeked of stink and menace barely contained.

At age seven, Little Pawlik experienced an early and abrupt introduction to sex education at the hands of Sal. Having had his head grabbed playfully in a vice-like grip with Sal's massive arms, the boy caught a nauseating whiff of the man's foul smelling whiskey breath. "How's that for a head lock, you little fart," bellowed the man, spewing forth saliva from his last swig. Twisting his face away to avert the miasma, the boy's eyes became glued to the exposed tattoo on Sal's massive, flabby left shoulder. He beheld large, uplifted breasts, the female figure's hips and buttocks posed at an erotically fetching angle, the hands coyly shielding the genitalia, the flesh-toned face displaying full red lips pouting a teasing come-hither look.

Somehow, even at the age of seven, he knew instinctively that Sal was no good for his mother, especially when he heard Sal address his mother — "you squaw bitch!" Hearing this biting expletive so often, he almost came to believe that it was his mother's given nickname.

Little Pawlik remembered seeing a drunken Sal on top of his nearly naked mother on the living room floor, holding her down, Linda screaming for the girls to do something. The sight of the man's huge torso leaning over his mom scared him even more than the two dagger tattoos on his right bicep and forearm, both entwined with snakes whose viper tongues lashed out between crimson red eyes.

When the shouting stopped, night would become quiet and Little Pawlik would crawl into bed beside his sister Susan, huddled against her warm body, she comforting him with a toy bear or a whispered story.

The evenings did not always go quietly. He remembered the secret things that Patricia Whitecloud whispered to Susan, the evil things that Sal did to her while she was in her bed at night. The boy's oldest half sister was just young and attractive enough to be tempting to this beast. Sal had threatened to kill Patricia, telling her she was supposed to tell no one.

But she couldn't help herself. Susan became Pat's confidante. And Little Pawlik became the innocent bystander who overheard these things that Sal did to Patricia's body.

Little Pawlik wondered if these things were normal, like the tattoo on Sal's shoulder. Even though Little Pawlik didn't understand what the touching meant, he knew something frightful had happened, because Patricia would tremble and the two young girls would hug and cry softly into the night. The boy would plug his ears, close his eyes and hope that sleep would forever erase these things.

He remembered, too, when his mother got really big around the belly, pregnant with Salvador Rodriguez' child. Her increasingly frustrated husband would come in late at night, drunk and raging, cussing and swearing and drinking even more.

One night, hearing screaming and banging from the kitchen, the boy got up from his bed and walked out into the hallway light. He saw the man strike his mother full in the face with his huge clenched fists, flexing the dagger tattoos on his bare, hairy arm. He never forgot the guttural, growling words — "fucking squaw bitch!" He saw the blood from his mother's broken, shattered nose splatter across the kitchen counter, dripping onto the floor, his mother sprawled under the table, screaming for her drunken husband to stop. Men came to the house that night and took his mother and Patricia Whitecloud away.

It was not until years later that Little Pawlik learned the terrible family secret. Not from Linda at first but from Doris. The man had sexually ravaged Patricia repeatedly and she had finally become pregnant with his child. Sam wanted to know why his mother hadn't bothered to tell him. To do something. Doris could only tell the boy that the man was an animal and that he had terrorized his mother for so long. She could never explain to the boy why his mother, at first, had been confused and jealous of Patricia Whitecloud — of her own daughter's intentions.

The boy next saw his mother, her broken, pregnant body, healing at the hospital. Doris had explained to him and sister Susan that their mother had serious, internal injuries. The starched white walls of the hospital room seemed such a contrast to her black-and-blue eyes and her silvery red, transparent skin covering the top of her broken nose. Linda spoke to her boy in whispers, her unsmiling swollen mouth and her blackened, puffy eyes turned up to him.

Linda told them, then, that he and Susan must go to live with Doris, her "trusted and close friend" for a spell, until she got well. Then she wanted to speak only to him, and Doris and Susan left the room. Little Pawlik felt alone. Linda Whitman smiled wistfully up at her son, then, and told him things. That she was tough and a survivor. That he needn't worry. That he needed to be brave, too. That he was becoming a man now. That she would try to bring a new brother or sister home to him.

This was the first time in Little Pawlik's life when he felt proud of his mother. And of himself for being of her blood.

Little Pawlik remembered the times when Doris Wallport would read to him, telling him wonderful stories about the Indians and about the Wild West. She told him all about his Nez Perce ancestors, and how they expertly raised and rode horses on the high, grassy meadowlands of the Wallowas. Doris bought him crayons and a coloring book full of horses. As he drew his multi-colored horses, he saw his favorite Nez Perce horses, Appaloosas and pinto ponies, running wild in the high mountain fields. Little Pawlik and his sister Susan would sit on the couch, draw more horses, and listen to those stories Doris Wallport told them for hours on end.

For the boy, Doris' stories became graceful, Wallowa mountain river falls, quenching his thirst for his heritage. She told him that he was different, that he and Susan were Indian and just as beautiful as other Anglo children. That they could be proud of their difference, proud that their skin was of darker complexion and that Sam's ancestors had lived in the Wallowas long before the white man had come.

Little Pawlik's mother, indeed, kept her promise, bringing him a new baby brother and a new apartment where they would stay. The place was typical of the low cost Section VIII public housing projects to which the boy had grown so accustomed — a two bedroom, one bath, small kitchen and tiny living room affair on the second story of a large, drab apartment complex just off Interstate 84 on the outskirts of Pendleton. Now Linda seemed to have found exclusive solace in caring for her new child, Roberto.

More anxious than ever for Linda to tell him the stories Doris had told, Little Pawlik felt excluded by his mother's preoccupation with his baby brother. And with her constantly going out to see friends. He and Susan continued to reassure each other, though, by recounting the stories Doris Wallport had told them.

Little Pawlik attended the same elementary school as Susan, she being three grades ahead of him. But school soon became a struggle for the child. Patricia Whitecloud no longer took care of him because she was gone. He was furious for reasons he did not know: at his mother's absences, at Patricia for being gone, at the attention Roberto got. The boy fought constantly. Somehow, Linda never seemed interested in what his teachers or the principal had to say, always taking him by the arm, bringing him home and leaving him there with his sister, only to return home hours later that evening. And sometimes not till the next day.

Little Pawlik wanted to know who he was, if Salvador Rodriguez was his father and what it meant to be Indian. But Linda had no time for his questions, only time to leave Susan, Roberto and him alone to fend for themselves.

It was at this time in the boy's young life that he first noticed that his mother's behavior exhibited a strangeness which Susan attributed to alcohol and the boy came to accept as normal. He decided that alcohol was something she needed to be normal.

As he grew older, Little Pawlik came to accept as normal, too, the fact that his mother finally had mustered the courage to divorce the man who had broken her nose while she was pregnant with Roberto. He was standing beside his mom the day the sheriff handed Sal the restraining order. The sheriff had told them that this piece of paper might provide his mother with protection from Sal.

Contrite when sober and even when served with the restraining order by the sheriff, Sal became sullen, then violent, the first time a shot of whiskey entered his system. Little Pawlik's mother had him arrested. The man finally left. But he would be back.

Linda kept the twelve-gauge shotgun hidden in her bedroom. The kids were instructed never to open their mom's closet next to the bed. She explained that she needed the gun to protect herself and Little Pawlik, his sister and his baby brother from Sal. "Nobody or nothin' will ever enter that closet, except me, if I need to — you unnerstan'?" she had boldly instructed. These words she had spoken to the boy and his sister, as they soberly promised to their mother never to look into or enter that forbidden zone. They did anyway.

Late one night, Little Pawlik's young life changed forever.

Sal, his voice raging, had followed the boy's mother home from a bar, breaking in through the front apartment door. The man's loud curses awoke Little Pawlik, causing the boy to shake in his bed. He had heard, countless times before, the crying screams from his mother and the low guttural sounds from the drunken man — "fuckin' squaw bitch!" The darkness in his room closing in on him from the times before came back again.

The corners and walls of his bedroom moved closer and closer — squeezing in on him — as the banging and screaming from outside grew even more shrill. The boy felt himself in the vice grip of the walls as the pandemonium reached a bedlam pitch. He saw shadowy lines pass through the light shining into his room from beneath his bedroom door, heard the crash of whiskey bottles breaking, saw the rushing of body shadows past his door. He heard the loud bang as his mother's bedroom door slammed shut against the force of the brutish man, his fists thundering against the door, the man screaming unutterable curses at his mother.

At eight years of age, Little Pawlik cowered beneath the sheets in his bed, curled in a fetal position, listening to the uproar from beneath his bed sheets, his wide-open eyes slowly peering into the darkness in his small ten-by-twelve-foot bedroom. He slowly lowered the bed sheets and looked out, exploring the corners of his room, the scream-ing and thunderous pounding of the fists coming back to him in waves, washing fresh fear into his blackened room. The boy wished that the darkness would envelop everything for him and shut out the sounds.

Then his eyes once more focused on the light from beneath his bedroom door. Strangely, inexorably, the light drew him out of his bed, through his fear, and over to the edge of the door. Should he open the door a crack and peer out? he wondered. Would the man curse at him? Would he see the daggers on his arm? Then he heard his mother's loud and commanding voice from within the bedroom, her bedroom door now apparently knocked open.

"Back up, man, and get the hell out," she screamed. "Or I'll blow you the fuck away!" The boy peeked out the door, now, and saw his mother, shotgun in hand, backing Sal, in underpants and undershirt, his bulging stomach sweaty with perspiration, back out into the kitchen. He watched him stagger backwards down the hallway, the barrel of the twelve-gauge shotgun unsteadily pointed at his chest, then at his stomach, then at his chest again. He heard the drunken, sweaty brute cursing — a broken whiskey bottle in his huge right hand.

Little Pawlik stepped out into the hallway behind his mother as she passed. He remembered how her head, her shoulders, her arms shook from fear.

"Get the fuck out of my place!" he heard his mother scream, her voice shaking with panic. "Don't ever come back, you bastard!" she faltered, then hesitated. Seeing this, the drunken man came at her. The man charged, his huge body surging with full force, jagged glass raised above the tattoos on his right arm, cursing, lunging at Linda Pawlik Whitman from the middle of the kitchen with his huge, raised fists.

Little Pawlik's singular memory of that evening, the most awful of his entire life, was hearing the explosive roar of the twelve-gauge shotgun going off, the barrel pointed directly into the perspiring gut of the oncoming man. The boy's ears rang. He screamed but could not hear his own voice and he fell backwards, flinching from fright.

In slow motion, he remembered seeing the man's outstretched arms, his torso blown backwards by the force of the gun blast. And yet it happened so fast that the boy never saw the man's stomach convulse and twitch as the metal shot entered his stomach and chest, his tissue and organs ripped and torn apart as they absorbed the boring metal pellets.

Seeing the man's body thrown backwards into the kitchen, the boy's heart pounded in convulsive bursts, his legs went numb. Slamming against the kitchen table and chair, Sal finally came to his resting place — propped grotesquely against the kitchen chair, like a puppet, arms and legs askew, slammed backwards by the force of the smoking blast.

And then, for the first time in his life, Little Pawlik heard high-pitched supplications from the man's mouth. Crying almost. It seemed such a sharp, weird contrast to the curses he had heard before, to the guttural, drunken bellowing of the brutish man.

"Oh God," he heard the man moan, the ringing from the blast now dwindling to a low reverberating hum in his ears. "Help me, please! Help me!" The man was staring at Linda, who was staring back at him, totally immobilized by the terror of it all. "Jesus, Linda, please help me!" That was the first and last time he had ever heard Sal address his mother using her given name.

Little Pawlik was a witness to all of these things. He saw where the force of the shotgun blast had blown and splattered pieces of the man's viscera, blood and tissue onto the smooth, yellow kitchen wall behind. A darker red than anything he had seen before slid silently down. The man's guts made the most horrible finger painting the boy had ever seen, as the gory ooze slid silently down the kitchen wall.

Everything was in slow motion.

He witnessed Sal's hands and jaw quivering and twitching involuntarily as if trying to gesture and say something to Linda all at once but not being able to make himself heard or understood. He witnessed the ends of the man's feet jerking repeatedly, in spastic involuntary motions, the result of a ripped spinal cord, its messages now being sent randomly from a brain which was quickly shutting down.

He witnessed the blood being expelled from the man's huge, perspiring body, now seeping and crawling from beneath him across the cracked white linoleum floor, a red viscous, thick mass slowly crawling and spreading under the kitchen table. And he heard, too, the high gurgle from the man's throat as he tried to say something and couldn't.

He noticed that his mother was no longer in front of him, having bolted from the room, screaming, everything still in slow motion.

He witnessed Sal's eyes. The earlier angry expression in those eyes was gone, in sharp contrast now with the supplicating, almost childlike look from the man's eyes. Then the man's eyes became glass. At first looking imploringly, directly at the boy, the pleading eyes, pupils still alive, slowly rose and stared at the yellow ceiling, innocent almost, searching for something — for some explanation.

The boy now heard his mother screaming and cursing incoherently. In the front room of the apartment she clutched her child, Roberto, in her arms and fled out the front door, stumbling from her own fright and intoxication down the stairs, out to the car below. Running to the front door, the boy heard the tires squeal and screech as the engine roared and the car hurtled violently onto the street in front of the apartments and sped off into the night. Linda — the man killer — somehow too drunk and panic-stricken to take Little Pawlik with her, to even stop and look for him or to acknowledge his presence, had left him behind.

Little Pawlik felt himself abandoned. Terrified, the boy forgot that Susan, too, was gone. Without thinking, the boy now rushed to the only place he had gone to before to seek safety — his bedroom, behind his bed. He had gone there so often before when he had been left alone. When Sal had raged there before.

From behind his bed, the apartment became quiet, almost ghost-like. Suddenly, the boy began to hear the man's low moaning sounds. He grew terrified, not understanding that the man's blood was now gushing from a ruptured aorta and useless lungs straining to breathe against the relentless invasion of death's process, causing a gurgling as the man slowly drowned in his own blood.

It seemed a ghoulish yet an almost natural kind of noise, but this time the finality to it terrorized him as never before. The death rattles made by Salvador Rodriquez — the last desperate attempts of a violent man's body to live and therefore to justify to itself that the person within was now about to die — was both wonderful and awful to Samuel Little Pawlik Whitman at that instant. Wonderful because of the realization that his mother was still alive; awful because he now knew that he, too, was mortal — just pieces of flesh and blood.

He stayed there, behind his bed, listening to the walls and the wind blowing cold outside. Disturbing noises reached him, the sounds of approaching sirens. Finally, a short, blue-uniformed police officer sporting a slight reddish brown beard came to the bedroom door, softly calling out his name. The officer's kindly, calm demeanor and look of authority reassured the boy. Little Pawlik noticed how big the officer's leather-holstered .45 caliber service revolver appeared, as he beckoned to the boy to come out. An eternity had passed.

The boy sprang from behind his bed through his bedroom door into the hallway, catching a final glimpse of the man's body and the upturned head once again. He stopped for an instant, catching a whiff of a putrid, tangy fecal odor. The boy did not realize that the nauseating smell emanated from the incontinence produced when the dying man's nervous system no longer could control sphincter and bladder muscles. Then he saw that the man's eyes had become forever still. The boy stared at those eyes he would never forget. Dead eyes. Veiny marbles in the man's head, now empty of life and set forever.

He ran past the twelve-gauge shotgun thrown on the living room floor by his mother and out through the front door, into the biting cold. People were standing in clusters outside now, strangers mostly — he couldn't find Susan.

His memory of that night and of the dark shadows it left would be everlasting. Little Pawlik would always feel the sting from that freezing cold February night, as he stood alone among strangers outside his mother's apartment on the second story balcony, watching the painful bright red lights and strange people's faces — at first frantic, then hurried, then sympathetic.

The darkness, the things he had witnessed and heard, had been Samuel Little Pawlik Whitman's battle, his war. He remembered the comfort he felt when a kindly woman wrapped a blanket around his shivering body and reunited him with Susan and then took them to a place he'd never been to before, a quieter place, surrounded by people he had never seen before.

But the terror which had gushed red hot within him that night would become a part of this little boy's inner life forevermore — a stain which Samuel Little Pawlik Whitman could never cleanse. The cold, quickly hardening mask of death had at once terrorized the boy and had also fascinated him. It had invaded the boy's soul in ways which not even he would ever completely comprehend.

CHAPTER 10

GREAT HORSE AND THE COLT

Time passed and Little Pawlik Whitman's stays with Doris Wallport resumed. Slowly, tentatively, the boy opened up. Doris helped him with his schoolwork and read him stories while his sister Susan played with Doris' daughter, Darlene. This way, they passed countless days.

The boy learned many things from Doris Wallport.

One evening Doris told him the story of how the great Chief Joseph had bravely fought and eluded the white man's army, but had finally surrendered, thirty miles from the safety of the Canadian border. Doris read to him the words Joseph had spoken to his people after the battle of Bear Paw Mountains, Montana in 1877:

"Our chiefs are killed....The old men are all dead....The little children are freezing to death....I want to have time to look for my children and see how many of them I can find. Maybe I can find them among the dead. Hear me, my chiefs. My heart is sick and sad. From where the sun now stands I will fight no more forever."

Little Pawlik heard and remembered the words of Thunder-Traveling-Over-the-Mountains; he took comfort that he was somehow descended from In-mut-too-yah-lat-lat, chief of the Wal-lam-wat-kin band of Chute-pa-lu, or as the Frenchmen called their people, the nose-pierced (Nez Perce) Indians.

Like Joseph's children, Little Pawlik too had been left alone in the world to freeze and had been left among the dead. As a witness to a violent death, the Indian child wondered if he too would "fight no more forever" or if the fighting instinct within himself would somehow keep him alive. He asked Doris about these things. He asked her if she knew who his father was. And she told him that he must someday talk with his mother.

Then one day Linda came home. Little Pawlik learned that Roberto was gone. Doris and Linda told the boy and his sister that their baby brother had gone away forever that terrible night — the night the shotgun had destroyed the child's father, Sal. Dim memories of one afternoon came back to the boy, when he and Susan were taken by Doris and his mom to an office where strangers in suits were present — when they talked about Roberto and the people explained why Roberto hadn't come back home. Carefully, they asked him questions about what he had seen that night. The only thing left for the boy was an emptiness within himself which he tried to fill with his own questions.

Little Pawlik tried to explain to his mother why he needed to know who his father was. That the freezing Nez Perce children had been found by their father, Chief Joseph. That this great chief had taken care of his children. "Will my father come and take care of me too?" he wondered aloud. "Mom?" he asked her. "Is my dad a great Indian? Does he have an Indian name?" Linda Whitman showed the boy a picture of Ron Hathaway from her high school yearbook. It was then that Little Pawlik learned that his father was an Anglo.

Why didn't he have the Hathaway name, he wondered. "Because Whitman is your heritage," his mother explained to him for the first time.

But who were the Whitmans? Were they Nez Perce? Did they know Chief Joseph? He asked Doris if she knew what Old Joseph had taught his son, Chief Joseph. What were the ways of his Indian ancestors? He wanted to know how Chief Joseph had led his children out of the Wallowa wilderness and how the white man had allowed them to come back, not to their native lands, permitting them, instead, to settle on the Nez Perce reservation in Idaho. He asked Doris to find their reservation on the map for him. "Where is Lapwai, Idaho?" he had asked.

Then one day Little Pawlik went to his mother and announced to her that his daddy had a name: Ron "Great Horse." It was then that Linda Whitman decided that she and Doris needed to talk.

"Why are you fillin' the boy's head with all this sentimental crap, Doris — that his ancestors were a bunch of goddamn heroes?" she asked one day while they were busy in Doris' kitchen. Linda was obviously displeased after hearing the boy repeat another one of the myths about his father. "I don't want this boy pretendin' he's got kinfolk who were supermen, a bunch of noble savages. That's bullshit!" she protested, irritated by Doris' well meaning meddling. To Linda, Doris' stories were naive and overwrought attempts to idolize her people. "Sam needs to know who his people really are," she stated emphatically.

"Listen, I had no idea you'd take offense." Trying to finish cooking a cheese omelet, Doris was taken aback that her friend's reaction wasn't one of total acceptance. "I'm sorry, girl. Just trying to teach the boy his Native American heritage. You know that."

"What heritage, gal?" Linda threw back with a scowl. "Broken promises? Bein' torn away from each other, our families?" She paused, trying to calm herself. "Your heritage lessons is assumin' a lot of things that may not be true," she continued, now glancing past Doris at the rising yellow omelet. "That's only gonna confuse him more. Don't you see? How can Sam live in the Anglo world and pretend he's still Indian? What tongue's he gonna learn? Cryin' out loud, girl. I want him to know the truth about his people," she protested, still unhappy but not taking her eyes off the omelet.

"What do you mean?" asked Doris, turning to face her friend.

"We gotta show him our ways today," said Linda. "I want my oldest son to be a survivor. Dammit, our people have to fend for themselves today," she went on, turning now and plunking herself down hard on the edge of a chair next to the formica-topped kitchen table. "There wasn't no crime and no drugs and all these cities and poverty in Joseph's day. Our people kept to themselves then. Just the woods and the mountains. Then the damn army threw us out. Good or bad, we've been thrown into an Anglo world and we have to learn to live with all kinds of folks. Sam needs to learn that."

Despite the distortions and myths spun from her well-meaning friend, Linda Whitman loved Doris. Doris had given a lot to Susan and Little Pawlik. It was more out of an overwhelming need to survive that Linda felt resentment. But deep within herself Linda was unsure how to communicate the need to survive to her oldest son.

"Well old gal," Doris finally replied, setting the omelet on the old table next to Linda, "let's you and I think of things we can do to show the kids their heritage."

"There you go, luv," beamed Linda, and they hugged. The proud Indian woman loved Doris Wallport for the way she so carefully diverted any anger that might have been produced by Linda's own vulnerability. They sat and ate the omelet together that afternoon, each knowing that Samuel Little Pawlik Whitman really needed to belong somewhere, to someone, to something.

* * * * *

The first time Little Pawlik felt that he really had a father was when he met his mother's new friend, Tony Aguilar.

A tall, happy-go-lucky dark-skinned Hispanic, Tony Aguilar was a trucker. The boy became fascinated with Tony and his wild stories.

"Hey, Sam, wanna know somethin' that really scared me on my last trip?" Tony asked the boy one evening. They were standing next to his truck, Samuel leaning against the broad chrome fender, palming and admiring the immense front tire.

"What happened?" the youngster asked, wide-eyed.

"Should'a been with me — was really somethin'," he paused. "Was drivin' a big load Tuesday night last week down this steep road into White Bird, Idaho. Was icy-cold. The road was inclined 'bout forty-five degrees." Tony tilted his arm as he spoke. The boy's mouth dropped open.

"What happened?" the boy gasped.

"Lost both my brakes, kid!" Tony paused again. "Kept my cool though," the man said as he raised his chin. "Tires were smokin like twin chimneys! Rig kept goin' faster and faster down the hill. Couldn't control 'er. Doin' about fifty-five or sixty."

"Wow!" cried the boy, his upturned head shaking with anticipation.

"Then I cranked up my ol' Jake brake — slowed 'er a little, but not much." He paused again. "It finally blew out. Boom!" he exploded, poking the boy in the stomach as the boy sprang back. "Then, just as I rounded this really sharp bend — really steep — I saw the truck comin' at me and the ramp."

"What ramp?" "What truck?"

"The runaway ramp, kid. Swung my rig off the road at the last second — just as the long truck passed me goin' up hill. My old rig hit that gravel ramp, and rocks just flew everywhere." Tony was swinging both arms wildly now. "Those runaway ramps go up hill pretty steep. My rig stopped right at the top."

"Wow!" The boy's wide dark eyes sparkled at the thought that his hero had kept his rig upright and his life intact.

Tony's rig, a towering Peterbilt eighteen-wheeler tractor-semitrailer with dual pipes and a sleeper in back, fascinated Samuel. He parked it next to the road in front of the apartment complex once a week when he was home. The boy lived for that truck. The tractor rig seemed two stories tall. Samuel loved touching the immense bumper on the front of the red and white tractor, gazing for long stretches at his face reflected in the wide, shiny chrome bumper.

The sleeper, or "box" as Tony called it, sat between the dual pipes and was the favorite of all the boy's retreats. He would beg Tony to show him how the CB worked. Tony cheerfully showed the boy how he chattered with other truckers — his call sign was "dingo-balls". Samuel learned to mimic the CB lingo. Tony showed him how the gears worked, let him touch the levers and even let him activate the horn.

The size of the truck and rasping boom of its horn made the boy feel powerful. As he sat high up in the huge cab, peering out at his sister below, he knew for sure he'd be a trucker. And a mechanic.

And he knew that Tony Aguilar was different from the other men his mother had known. For one thing, he rarely drank. This good-natured man had known Linda since grade school in Pendleton. Drifting in and out of her life, Tony had rescued his mother. At least that's how Samuel saw it.

One hot day in July, Tony Aguilar drove all of them in his air-conditioned rig up to Chief Joseph days, a week long cowboy and Indian festival hosted by Joseph, a little Oregon town near Wallowa Lake. That summer time for Little Pawlik was strange and wonderful. For the first time he actually saw his mother happy. Linda Pawlik had lost weight and was beautiful and radiant with her long, glowing black hair. She wore her rainbow dresses and golden blouses, bedecked in beaded, multi-colored jewelry.

Doris knew that the boy might never be taken to the traditional Nez Perce festivities held on the reservation or in the tiny Idaho towns of Lapwai, Kamiah and Craigmont. So, despite Linda's admonitions, she filled Little Pawlik's head with all of the wonderful tribal legends and of heroic Indian deeds, explaining that his tribe still held war-dance contests and Indian games.

Then Little Pawlik went to visit Old Joseph's grave near Wallowa Lake. The boy thought of his father's image in the high school year-book and what his mother had once told him — that he was an Anglo.

"Mom?" he had asked her plaintively. "Why did my dad leave? Why can't I see him?" Linda had looked at her little boy's imploring face a long time and had finally answered.

"Your dad left like all the other men, Little Pawlik," she had replied. And the boy had accepted this, too, as normal.

Now he stood next to his mom and Susan and Doris at Old Joseph's grave. The tall, light gray stone column, surrounded by dried flowers, beads, paper trinkets and talismans, rested atop the grassy knoll just north of Wallowa Lake. The boy marveled at how the snowcapped Wallowas reflected off the glassy lake surface, whispering still beneath a burning sun. Little Pawlik stared at the words etched into the stone.

"Your grandpa, you know, was named Joseph," Linda told him. "Joseph Pawlik."

"Yeah — Doris told me once," Little Pawlik replied. Linda's glance at her friend found a knowing smile on Doris' lips.

"Joseph Pawlik was quite a man. Used to ride horses and rodeo at the Pendleton roundup," Linda continued. Her son, examining one of the stone talismans off to the side, looked up, first at his mom, then at Doris.

"He was a real cowboy?" he asked.

"Yup," said Doris proudly. "Rode the wild bulls like no one else." Little Pawlik returned to examining the talisman. It was a stone horse. Looking at the thing, Little Pawlik decided that his father's absence simply meant that his dad, like his grandfather Joseph Pawlik, was a more revered, mythical person.

Knowing his ancestors had raised horses high in the Wallowas, Little Pawlik pictured Ron Hathaway seated atop his coal black Appaloosa stallion, with his dark hair, firm cleft chin, a direct look and brave, erect bearing.

Ron "Great Horse" Hathaway, the horseman, the cowboy and the hero, was made from great stuff — a comforting myth for the boy. The image drowned out the fact that, up to now, Little Pawlik's life had been a long parade of missing persons from Patricia Whitecloud to Sal to Roberto — as well as other men he had met from the bars and truck stops who had come and gone.

Then Linda and Tony Aguilar had their first and only baby, a boy they named Sandy. Little Pawlik felt his mother grow distant again. Left to wondering alone, Little Pawlik at first decided that he was really more Indian — like his half sister Susan — or part Indian and part Hispanic like his little half brother Sandy. But could Ron Hathaway be part Hispanic? What was it like to be Anglo? The answers were as elusive as the lightning quick stallions and pinto ponies that ran high in the Wallowa meadowlands.

* * * * *

With time, the myth of Ron "Great Horse" slowly melted away. Little Pawlik would seek out his mother. She would be gone. His questions went unanswered. Except one day when she finally told him, somewhat off-handedly, that she thought that "it might be a good idea to go downtown and visit Hathaway Hardware Store."

After weeks of thought and hesitation, the boy finally resolved to visit The Store himself — perhaps he might see or even meet his biological father.

Living in a small apartment on the outskirts of Pendleton meant that they never got into town that much. Catching a bus and going downtown was a new experience for the ten-year-old boy.

As he opened the old wooden-framed glass door beneath the sign "Hathaway Hardware and Sporting Goods", a bell rang. Samuel felt a strange tightening in his chest. He peered inside the cramped front entrance. A musty smell of old hardwood and leather reached him as he saw rows of fishing rods stacked against the yellow rear wall. To the immediate front and right was a glass counter packed with knives, glistening lures, rainbow flies and other fishing paraphernalia. To the left, against the wall, rested the canoes and boats. He went there.

Walking slowly, the boy marveled at the shapes and sizes of the drift boats, all inflated, all with strange names and decorated red and black, gold and white. He reached out and traced with his finger the edge of a yellow decal glued to the top of one of the inflated outer chambers.

"Can I help you, young man." The woman's voice from behind startled him. Turning, the boy beheld the big, good natured woman's green and white plastic name tag: "Betty."

"Is - is - Ron - Mr.- - Ron Hathaway — is he here?" the Indian boy stammered.

The big woman studied the Indian boy. No one spoke. "Why no," she finally answered. "Do you need to see him?" The Indian boy stood mute. "He doesn't live here anymore," she said, smiling down at the boy. "Can someone else help you?"

Little Pawlik's dark eyes stared up at the big woman. "Just thought he'd be here, is all," he said, his voice trailing off to a whisper.

The big woman looked perplexed. She noticed the boy trembling. "Do you need anything honey? Are you lost?" Little Pawlik looked at the floor and made no reply.

"Guess I'll be goin' now," he finally mumbled, at once glancing up at the woman's face and turning to go.

Ron Hathaway's mother looked at the Indian boy as he left. She stood there by the door a long time after the door closed.

Pi-Nee-waus Days was held that year in August at Lapwai. Little Pawlik got to ride over in Tony's sleeper, when he wasn't at his side in the cab listening to his hero work the CB and watching him downshift his big rig. Little Pawlik totally forgot about The Store. The parades, war dances, Indian games and Nez Perce tribal exhibits became his new world. Little Pawlik felt stirrings inside of him he'd never experienced before. Seeing the people, their celebrations, and their animals, he remembered Chief Joseph Days and the Wallowas again — and the pinto ponies and the stories Doris had told him.

A warmth entered the boy, a deep conviction that he was a part of a larger group of dark-skinned peoples — his people — who somehow knew how to live and survive. Pride entered Little Pawlik, now, and took its place along with the terror and confusion which for so long he had taken for granted as a normal part of his existence.

Then Tony Aguilar disappeared.

At age eleven, Sam finally learned that grades and homework were meaningless chores for other kids and that his fists were lightning quick.

The constant teasing at school, especially about his unusual protruding ears — "dumbo," "space cadet," "cauliflower brains" — made the boy ever more aware that he was different. Quickly, his fists separated him even more. The little boy who had struggled and fought with himself for so long, now fought others. And eventually the authorities. His poor history became a rambling trail of having to survive the damage he caused to others when provoked. It was as if he could barely contain the raging and boiling from within — a kind of mutant, cross-cultural virus that grew, yet seemed to protect him in a way that nothing else could.

* * * * *

Before Samuel's twelfth birthday, he left Pendleton with his mother and his baby brother and moved to Eugene, where Doris Wallport had settled a year earlier with her youngest daughter.

With Doris' help, Samuel's mother attended community college under a grant, taking bookkeeping classes while working as a clerk for a Head Start program and later at an Urban Indian Center.

Starting over with these new experiences helped the Indian woman talk to her son more about his heritage. He was a Native American — an Indian — she told him, and must be a true survivor. But he must also be tough because he was an Anglo.

Still, the kids at school sensed the boy's weaknesses. And when they pounced, they found an arrogant, angry young man always ready to fight back. He was like his mother had told him to be, a survivor and tough.

The fat, silvery ring inserted through Samuel Little Pawlik's left ear lobe at age thirteen signified a rite of passage, an act of bravado, which was as much a part of his identity — his heritage — as the rings he thought were worn by his nose-pierced Indian ancestors. He was proud.

In Eugene, his one constant friend — his associate — who Sam's mother detested, was a hard street kid named Tom Strickler. The appeal for Sam was Tom's older, swaggering attitude. And the older boy challenged the younger boy to take dangerous chances, to defy the easy way, the straight way, the sissy way.

That's why having a gun, now, appealed so much to Sam. It seemed at first that when the ringing had finally stopped in his head from that shotgun blast, he had wanted to utterly blot out any memory of that night and the protection his mother had kept in the closet.

And yet Samuel couldn't help but remember. He never stopped hearing the blast for even one day. He was fascinated with the sheer power of the thing. After all, he had witnessed it all — the gun blast had blown with such force into the man's belly. How utterly helpless and ruined the huge, ugly man had looked, his life oozing away in a thick smear of blood spreading outward from under the kitchen table.

Sam's first gun was one he stole with his friend Strickler one warm Friday evening in early August. The Strickler kid had purchased several six-packs and they spent the evening cruising the back streets of Eugene and then Springfield. Seated together in Strickler's two-door Ford sedan overlooking a darkened old farm house at 12:30 in the morning, Strickler pulled a plastic bag from under the driver's seat.

"Ya want one?" Strickler asked, holding the bag of greenish brown vegetation in front of the boy's face. The blond boy's wide jaws were set like a pit bull's, teeth clenched, as if hatching a plan. He plucked out a large pinch from the bag, carefully licked the brown paper, and rolled a fat joint between his fingers.

"Wha's it like?" Sam asked, feeling the dizzying effects of the booze.

"Makes ya mellow out —- relaxes ya," the older boy replied. "All my friends smoke weed," he added nonchalantly.

"Na, think I'll pass."

"Ah come on, don't be a chickenshit, kid," protested the older boy, "'Sides, the weed's just like the peyote stuff your Indian relatives toke up on all the time."

Half an hour later, Sam was following the blond kid towards the back of the still darkened farmhouse where the older boy suggested they would go "have some fun." Seeing the dilapidated screen door so close up seemed unreal to Sam — like high stakes exploring for lost treasure.

Strickler quickly turned the back door knob and the door opened with a squawk. Entering behind his friend, Sam peered out, letting his eyes adjust to the blackness of the large kitchen. He was barely able to make out the old refrigerator and gas stove. He jarred into the hard oak table in the middle of the kitchen.

"Careful, kid," Strickler whispered. "Let's see if we can find us some silverware or jewelry or somethin'." Moving into the living room, Sam made out the outlines of an old piano. Seeing the stairs, he strode to the top and saw the bedroom door ajar. Numbed as if in a trance, the boy entered what seemed like the inner sanctum. Each step brought faint squeaking from the tight floor boards. He carefully approached the elaborately carved walnut jewelry box atop the old dresser next to the curtained window. Glancing down at the half-opened drawer, he rifled through and beneath the fluffy underclothes, handkerchiefs and stockings. His fingers touched the hard, cold steel of the barrel and froze. The floor squeaked. Someone was standing behind him.

"What'd ya find?" came the slurred whisper. Sam slammed into the dresser, catching himself with an outstretched hand on the mirror. He glanced up. Behind him, reflected in the mirror, stood Strickler.

"Ya scared the fuck outta me, god damn it!" Sam almost yelled.

Strickler reached past the boy into the drawer under the clothes and pulled out a Colt .45 automatic pistol. The moon's glow through the bedroom window gave the thing a smooth and menacing sheen. "Well, look what the fuck we have here, kid!" Strickler's eyes narrowed to slits as his wide jaws broadened into a grin. "Hold out your hand, kid," he instructed. Sam did as he was told. "Your first piece. Your first fuckin' Colt," he laughed. "Take good care of it." As Sam grabbed the barrel, he looked at his friend. The mention of Colt made the boy think at once of the wild Wallowa horses Doris had helped him draw. "Don't grab the god damn thing by the barrel, you idiot," Strickler annoyingly lectured again. "Pick it up by the handle." Tensing, Sam shifted the .45 to his other hand.

"Boom!" A mind-jarring twitch blew through him in an instant. The bullet tore through the floor not six inches from the older boy's foot.

When they finally reached the Ford sedan parked up the street, Sam's ears were still ringing. Slouched into the seat next to his friend, he noticed that the Colt .45 was still attached to his right hand, more real to him now than the horses he had drawn so long ago. And so powerful.

Bolt upright and glassy eyed, Strickler turned on the ignition, leaving the lights off. "Better get the fuck outta here man! Here comes the owner!" Glancing back, Sam noticed an old battered Ford pickup idle slowly up to the side of the farmhouse. Strickler's sedan inched forward. A man and a woman got out of the pickup cab. A large dog and two young boys jumped out of the back end. The sedan, with its two occupants, quietly inched away.

Feeling Strickler's sedan accelerate, the boy became lost in blurry thought. Like his mother before him, Sam figured he needn't account to anyone why he would keep his Colt. And, like his mother, it was definitely no one's business to know where he kept it.

The gun was Sam's power projected and connected him to a frightening secret he had kept locked within himself — the power and awesome bloodiness of the deadly violence he had beheld. It seemed such a normal thing. Violence had protected his mother from the violence. Had ended it. Now, he decided, a gun would protect him from the mocking and abuse of others.

To prove himself as a man, Sam had decided, was the ultimate rite of passage for him, was much more important than school. Conformity to an ordered Anglo world made little sense. Nor did Chief Joseph's pledge make sense — to "fight no more forever." Little Pawlik had now grown up after all and had learned the lesson well — the one his mother had spoken to Doris about — how she had wanted her boy to learn to be a survivor. But with a gun, because that seemed to be his heritage.

* * * * *

The three of them, Linda Whitman, Samuel, and Doris Wallport, had been sitting in the stuffy, drab second floor office of the Support Enforcement Division that rainy April afternoon for fifteen minutes listening to the incessant ring of the phone and watching the frantic gestures of the few female clerks who worked behind the wooden counter. Sam, sullen and bored, was slouched in a chair, head resting back, dozing off. A clerk motioned to Linda to come up to the counter.

"I'm sorry you've had to wait so long, ma'am. But Mr. Jacobs, our investigator, is a little behind today," the slender, pleasant-mannered woman explained apologetically. Linda nodded slowly.

"No, problem, ma'am," said the Indian woman with quiet dispassion. "Been waitin' his whole life!" She motioned her head towards Sam, then glanced down at the counter, averting the female clerk's attentive look. "A few more minutes wait ain't gonna' matter to me none," she added, shrugging her large shoulders. The polite female clerk, in her early fifties, looked at the Indian woman, vaguely wondering why her particular problem had taken so long to fix and why she seemed so patient.

Linda turned away and proudly walked back to her seat, sat down beside Doris Wallport and continued occupying herself with a "Woman's Day" magazine. Becoming bored with the magazine, she tossed it onto the small table full of year-old, worn magazines in the center of the small waiting room. She leaned over and whispered to Doris for the list tucked in the front pocket of Doris' white coat perched on her lap.

Sam, barely awake, glanced and noticed how his mother held her head up, noticed the proud, set profile of her jaw, noticed how her lips moved slowly as she carefully read the crumpled white paper retrieved from Doris' coat pocket. He felt a swelling of pride for his mother.

Glancing at the "Road and Track" magazine he now held in his hand, Sam was reminded how much pride he took in his mother's huge, four-door, ancient Olds. The "whale", as he called it, was a tottering, battered, dinosaur of a car. He had kept the wreck running for his mother way past its prime. Tony Aguilar had taught him all about how engines and spark plugs and pistons worked. Sam knew how to change the oil, knew how to check the brake linings, knew how to examine the radiator for leaks, and how to do all the things you needed to do to keep the engine running — or at least tell a trusted mechanic what might be wrong. His intense interest in that old "whale" had saved his mother countless trips to the service station or useless mechanical expenses for a car that was just barely running and shouldn't have even rightfully been allowed on the road. The thing had hauled them all to Eugene.

Looking at his mother, now, intently reading her list, he smiled as he thought of how that morning he had unclogged the toilet filled with pieces of plastic toys stuffed there by Sandy, and the way his mother had applied the brakes to the Olds in the parking lot outside.

Little Pawlik noticed the small patches of hair missing from her head, her dark-complexioned, pockmarked cheeks and jagged nose. Her nose had always reminded him of the abuse and violence she had taken. The boy felt a pride in the very flaws that were a part of his mother, a pride that seemed to soothe the emptiness within himself. She was a survivor and so was he.

CHAPTER 11

THE GUMSHOE

The immense man sitting on top of the small swivel chair caused it to squeak and groan beneath him. He was hunched over the table, elbows in front of him and palms on either side of his massive jowls, his flowing gray hair reaching below his collar. His beard, matted with sweat, framed his large, slightly protruding forehead dotted with beads of sweat. His dark eyebrows arched as his brown eyes squinted at the massive file in front of him. He slowly turned the pages with the stubby index finger of his right hand, breathing slightly labored. This gentle giant of a man had been studying the case history of Linda Pawlik and her youngster, Samuel Whitman, with a commitment that bordered on the devotion he poured into his own family.

Jessie Lamont Jacobs had a real affinity for uniting runaway kids with their parents, or simply providing shelter or counseling for them. More of an outgrowth from his job as an investigator for the Department of Justice, this "hobby interest" of his — as he called it — was perhaps a bit too altruistic. Georgia would sometimes needle him for "spending too much time with those kids and not enough time with your daughters." But Georgia's gentle chiding was prompted more by a protective instinct for Jessie than as an excuse to nag him.

Georgia first met Jessie in the basement cafeteria of the State Office Building one afternoon, eating lunch. A single mother, she was immediately attracted to Jessie not so much because of his Gargantuan appetite — she liked food too — but for his quiet and unobtrusive ways. To her, this enormous man seemed to be genuinely self-deprecating in a warm, comfortable, yet confident sort of way.

And Jessie loved them both — her and her daughter Ashley Louise, whose father had long since dropped out of the picture. Jessie adopted Ashley shortly after they were married. Probably because of his high-school basketball days, Jessie took such pride in coaching Ashley.

Later, Georgia marveled at how her husband always seemed to find the time to play with their own two teenage daughters. Listening to Jessie's stories so often, everyone knew their names. Marci Lorraine and Traci Lynn. Even now, Jessie loved to coach girls basketball with Warren, Ashley's husband and father of Jessie's granddaughter, seven-year-old Becky Ann. One more granddaughter had recently joined the team, three-month-old Natalie Louise. The big bearded grandfather insisted that they present the baby with official tiny Nike tennis shoes at the hospital.

Georgia loved Jessie because she knew he genuinely cared about kids so much and hated to see them "fall through the cracks." He would tell her about the ones that went the wrong way. And about the ones he could reach. Georgia knew it hurt him inside when a kid of his got into trouble.

Perhaps this is why Jessie gabbed so incessantly about sports, chattering constantly about the games his girls played and how he, too, was involved in overseeing their every move. Actually, Jessie wasn't the only one involved. He had seen to it that Georgia never missed one of his daughter's or granddaughter's basketball games. She would bring refreshments and help keep "stats." Jessie could tell you about his team's basketball "stats," in detail, for what seemed like hours on end.

Jessie Jacobs let out a heaving sigh and pushed his belly away from the table, chair squeaking beneath his immensity. Rubbing his eyes slowly, he looked down between his knees, lost in thought. His job as Chief Investigator for Support Enforcement Division, with the Oregon Department of Justice, had taken him away from his home a lot. He had responsibility for a large territory. Two days a week he was at the office in Portland. He was able to stay in Salem, his hometown, one or two days a week. He traveled to Eugene the rest of the time.

Ten years ago at a planning meeting in Salem he had been told that budgetary constraints were such that staff shortages were inevitable and that he must handle investigations for the entire Willamette Valley.

As he sat this Thursday afternoon in the drab, poorly lit inner sanctum of his office, in a run-down building rented by the state of Oregon, this public servant, now in his mid fifties, reflected over the nearly three decades he had been an employee with the state of Oregon.

First he had worked as a clerk, right out of the Army, with the Department of Revenue. That job bored him to death, and he'd sought a transfer after six months, finally moving over to the Department of Commerce as a clerk in the Corporation Commissioner's Office. That job was no easier to cope with either.

Jessie always yearned to be a social worker, but didn't have the credentials. Newly married, with an adopted baby girl, he moonlighted at Chemeketa Community College and later Oregon State University while working days for the state.

Finally Jessie got his degree in social work with a minor in communications. He wanted more than anything to land a job with Children's Services Division but had to settle, instead, for a slot with the Support Enforcement Division. He remembered how he wondered, at first, what this agency did, what possible good it would serve chasing after errant parents, mostly fathers, who never paid support. Working his way along over the years, he went from intake specialist to investigator, and finally, five years ago, was promoted to Chief Investigator for the region. It had been explained to him that the promotion was a plum. But to Jessie, the plum didn't have too much to show for it in terms of financial remuneration. The promotion had been a mixed bag.

The bureaucracy, the paperwork and the "bullshit snafus" as he called them, were all part of the drudgery. But the positive side of his job also freed him to give a part of himself to those who could use his help — the runaway kids he counseled from all over western Oregon.

He remembered the meeting of his Lutheran Church discussion group that Sunday, ten years ago. The topic was the problem of runaway teens. Jessie led the discussion and the minister offered a challenge to him then: "Instead of talking about the problem, why don't we do something about it?" the minister had asked. Something inside of Jessie just clicked. After talking with a few of his friends, he studied the problem some more, then started visiting drop-in centers. Finally, Jessie and three of his friends from church decided to commit themselves to this permanent church project, a ministry really.

Organizing its own Lutheran Counseling "Drop-In" Center in Salem, Jessie's church began offering counseling and a network of support for runaways. The idea quickly took hold at Lutheran churches in Eugene and even Portland.

Eight years of weekend counseling activities, providing foster shelter for troubled kids and prodding the agency to cooperate in locating runaways had made the big man somewhat of a father figure to a lot of kids. And an occasional thorn in the side of the agency. But Jessie didn't really care, and the agency didn't seem to mind either, as long as it didn't affect the budget.

Jessie's co-workers, though, never could quite understand how this king-weighty man found both the time and energy to coach his girls, counsel the runaway kids and still perform his job as Chief Investigator — a job which required a mountain of reading.

The big man leaned back in his swivel chair and rubbed his tired eyes. For the past forty-five minutes, he had been methodically reading Linda's public assistance case file. This afternoon he was not a government employee merely going through the motions. He had taken extra pains with this case. He had spent the previous evening reading through Linda's "other" file: the Children's Services Division social file.

Unable to understand the dawdling in Sam's paternity case, Jessie's hunch was that the temporary removal of Linda's children from her custody might provide a clue — a reason for the agency's long delay. Jessie's experience with kids had made him adept at reading between the lines. The case history and social files were clinical and emotionless. Jessie Jacobs could figure out, though, that this woman had been through a hell of a lot.

Beaten, battered and abused by several men, she had suffered through her oldest daughter being sexually molested. And she had shot her first husband, Salvador Rodriguez, to death. She had been charged with murder and pled guilty to involuntary manslaughter. The public defender had evidently convinced the district attorney in Pendleton that the shooting had been self-defense. It seems the boy, Sam, had been the crucial and the only other eyewitness. The same night Linda had shotgunned her husband to death, she had fled to her friend Doris Wallport's place and had been involved in a motor vehicle fatality. Hysterical and intoxicated, she had careened, with the baby Roberto in the front seat, into a cement abutment on the way. The child had died two days later from head injuries and a punctured lung.

In the back of his mind, as he carefully flipped through the pages of the social and case history, Jessie wondered whether this kid would eventually turn to the streets or stay with this mother. And he wondered if the youngster had accompanied Linda here today.

He got up slowly from his chair, stroking his sweaty gray beard with his right hand and turned, reaching out with his thick, pale fingers for the doorknob. Swinging his six-foot-two frame upright, he let out a quiet belch from deep within his huge overhanging belly. He opened the door and stood there, peering out into the waiting room from behind the counter. Across the hazily lit room, he saw the Indian woman seated in her chair, a piece of white paper held across her large stomach with both hands, her head bowed, eyes closed. To her right, sat another portly woman, fortyish, wearing brown slacks, a white coat perched on her lap, intently reading a magazine. To her right was slouched a sullen-looking teenager, shiny ring in his left ear lobe, baseball cap on backwards, reading "Road and Track" magazine.

Jessie glanced at his watch. It was now 4:00 in the afternoon. The office was supposed to close at 5:00 P.M. He had arisen before sunup and had started work before 7:00 that morning.

Tired, Jessie threw out his great arms as he opened his mouth in a wide yawn, his green-checkered flannel shirt stretching at the buttons, nearly bursting open at the stomach. As he slowly arched his back, his white suspenders expanded. Hyperflexed in this position, the bearded man resembled a huge ceremonially decorated bow, half-drawn, from which unceremoniously hung a pair of baggy brown trousers, descending to half-hidden immense black leather shoes. "Real gunboats" he liked to refer to them. Letting himself relax, he strode over to the drinking fountain on the wall to his right. For a man with his 300-pound frame, Jessie's gait was notably soft. He wore gigantic-sized fourteen, triple wide, thick rubber-soled Rockport shoes. As he leaned over for a drink he noticed that though his feet felt comfortable, his back was sore. Straightening up with a wince, he reminded himself that he needed to readjust his chair pillow to ease the constant pain in his back caused by the pull from his huge belly. Glancing down at the tops of his shoes again, his mouth broke into a smile. The humorous notion that he was, as others had said, "the quintessential government gumshoe," pushed away the back pain he had felt moments before.

Jessie Jacobs was, in all his immensity, a tremendously self-assured man who was not threatened in the least by the jibes of others. His self-deprecating, self-effacing manner told everyone — especially kids — not to be over-awed by his size.

Jessie motioned to Mandy Tugman, the desk clerk, to come over. Wide-eyed, she approached him, almost on tiptoes. He seemed to her a bearded Jolly Green Giant. Jessie was now ready to conduct his last daily session late that April afternoon.

A slender wisp of a woman in her early fifties, Mandy's kindness, warmth and sympathy for others ran completely counter to the vague notion that bureaucrats and government clerks are all callous, disinterested and gruff automatons. But despite her asthma, this frail woman was strong-willed, too. Soft spoken, with a disarming giggle, she had the patience and gentleness to calm many a rude caller. She had the ability to be firm with Jessie too, a man three times her size, when he was tardy such as this afternoon.

"Jessie," she politely but nervously scolded him. "That nice lady and her boy over there have been waiting for over an hour." Mandy looked up at Jessie's dark, baggy eyes, swollen from reading. Her mild scowl turned to a grin. "You should be ashamed of yourself," she chided, giggling nervously while awaiting a response from Jessie.

"Well then Mandy, would you kindly have Ms. Aguilar and her youngster come on back — I'm ready," he said, obviously weary from all the reading but grinning down at her nonetheless. She hurriedly complied, going to the counter and announcing to the folks, with an apologetic giggle, that the investigator had been very busy and that he would now meet with Linda and her son. Seeing that Linda was sound asleep, the woman next to her gave Linda a firm nudge and whispered to her. The wait was finally over.

Turning, Jessie slowly ambled back inside the room like a bear retreating into its den. He turned back towards the door, adjusted the pillow on his swivelling chair and stood by the edge of the table, his hands on the stack of files he had been reading and studying intently. Jessie Jacobs stood there waiting for the Indian woman and her child to enter.

CHAPTER 12

THE INTERVIEW

H
ello, ma'am. I'm Jessie Jacobs, the support investigator assigned to your paternity case." Jessie took the Indian woman's hand in a firm shake, noticing her tired eyes — which she kept lowered — and the ridge of her prominent, broken nose. He noticed, too, that she gave him only half her hand. Glancing back over her shoulder to the left, he caught the shy grin of the tall lanky youngster with the silvery ring through his left ear lobe. The kid seemed quiet, withdrawn in a way he'd seen other teenagers, but noticed that the boy's handsome physical appearance seemed to belie his shyness. Dark complexioned with small pimples on his cheekbones and a high-ridged nose, a crop of longish, unkempt black hair sprang from beneath his cap. "You must be Sam," Jessie said warmly to the boy.

"Yeah, hello sir," the boy muttered awkwardly, looking down and around to the nearest chair. Finding one in the corner of the drab inner room, he walked over to it, plunking himself down in the chair next to a table with the same dated magazines he'd found in the waiting room an hour earlier.

"Just call me Jess, son," he said to the boy, looking directly at him now. Jessie always liked to start things on an informal note, especially with teenage kids who felt awkward. Sam looked up and gave Jessie a tired, crooked smile. Sam's look bothered him. The youngster seemed groggy, disoriented. Jessie realized immediately that the kid was profoundly bored with it all. Perhaps, he thought, Sam might even be making silent fun of his portly 300-pound frame tucked beneath his white suspenders, balanced delicately beside the table in the middle of the room.

Jessie motioned for Linda to be seated in the chair opposite him next to the table. He eased his huge bulk back onto the tired swivelling chair, the chair protesting again, the soft pillow positioned, this time, a little higher up in the small of his back. Out of the corner of his eye, Jessie caught the boy's crooked grin growing wider. Turning his attention back to Linda, he noticed that the boy's mother did not seem amused with either his portly frame nor did she seem especially warmed by the introduction.

"I'll get right to the point," Jessie began, sensing what he thought was Linda's impatience. "I am coming into this thing late in the game. Our agency first became acquainted with you when your oldest daughter, Patricia, was born. Our office in Pendleton was handling your claim and your grant, then. I have been able to review the office records from Pendleton up until the time you left there and came to Eugene," he explained in his usual methodical manner. "The files also made reference to the fact that your children had to be removed several times from your care because of circumstances beyond your control," Jessie said politely. Jessie explained to Linda that he had done his homework, telling her that he had thoroughly reviewed records from the Children's Services Division as well as the public assistance records. He concluded by complimenting Linda that she had overcome a tremendous amount simply to survive. But Jessie's attempt at flattery did not warm Linda.

"What does that have to do with my paternity case?" Her curtness and downcast stare told Jessie that this proud but private woman was in no mood for polite, idle chatter.

"Nothing, ma'am, other than to explain that things have perhaps taken so long because of your family's circumstances, and all," he explained. Pausing, Jessie looked over at the boy who seemed to be looking around the room. "Do you want to come over here and sit at the table, son?" he asked.

"Dunno-guess so," he nervously stated, glancing furtively at his mother, seeming to search for the right answer. Linda refused to divert her glare from her lap.

"He knows why he's here today, Mr. Jacobs. He knows this is about his father, Ron Hathaway."

"Good, then let's get started," said Jessie. "Just have a few questions and some explaining to do before I let you go." The Indian woman gave him a quick, skeptical look. She glanced down at the white, lined paper she held in her lap, below the edge of the table and Jessie's line of sight. But Jessie knew instinctively what she was holding. Like so many mothers before her, she seemed to be guarding her list of questions, which had been so carefully prepared for this moment.

"A friend 'a mine prepared some questions for me to ask," the Indian woman began slowly. Looking at the first of Doris' questions, Linda asked rather tentatively, "Why is this thing takin' so long?" She glanced back up from the paper without looking at Jessie. Her gesture told him that she was miffed at the way the agency had handled things and he listened patiently. He knew this woman didn't want to hear excuses. "You know, there was a meetin', a long meetin', seven or eight years ago in Pendleton. They asked me all these questions about Hathaway, about our relationship, and all those things." She glanced back down at the paper. "Told me we was gonna have blood tests and everything. I waited for them to contact me, but no one did. I even called once or twice. Said they couldn't find my file the first time." Linda paused, now, and laughed out loud. "Jesus, next time I called no one could answer my questions. I just sorta gave up, ya know. Figured they weren't interested or nothin'." The intensity of Linda's look, her simple honesty, was not so much disturbing to Jessie as it was embarrassing.

"Ms. Aguilar, I can't really tell you why nothing was done sooner to establish your youngster's paternity," answered Jessie apologetically

"Whoah! Aguilar?" The woman gave Jessie a startled look as she leaned back in her chair. "Name's Whitman, now, not Aguilar," she corrected him. "Geez, maybe that's why it's taken so damn long. You guys lost my last name." The thought amused her enough to provoke a slight smile at the edges of her mouth.

"Don't think so, ma'am," retorted Jessie. "File here says your maiden name's Whitman, sure enough. Then Rodriguez. Then Aguilar." He smiled back at her. "Did you legally change your name back to Whitman when you and Mr. Aguilar divorced?" he asked.

"Nope," came her reply. "Just prefer usin' the name Whitman, again. Had enough trouble usin' other men's names. Just prefer my own, I guess." Sensing that the subject at hand had gotten off track, Linda pressed Jessie for an answer. "So why wasn't Sam's paternity thing done sooner?" she asked again.

"All I can say is that when you came over here from Pendleton a while back, your case file was not transferred from the Pendleton office to our Eugene office." Jessie paused, taking in a breath. "It seems things kind of fell through the cracks. Because we have such a big caseload, these things happen, you know." The big man was trying to reassure the Indian woman, looking directly at her, now, seeking approval for the answers he tried to give her. The woman refused to look at him. Samuel Whitman was dozing off.

"No, Mr. Jacobs, I don't know," she replied slowly, deliberately. "There just doesn't seem to me to be any good reason why this thing has gone on for so long, and I really don't need to listen to a lot of excuses," she added. "I'm tired. I just came in here today 'cause I got

105

this letter you sent me and I want to get this thing over with. We've all been sittin' out there in your waitin' room." Linda kept her eyes lowered, her glare pressing into the table, then her lap. "I think you owe it to the boy now and you owe it to me too," she stated emphatically. "I need support from this man."

"Good," replied Jessie, trying to sound upbeat. "That's why we're here." Jessie paused a second and prefaced his remarks with care. "Ms. Whitman," he began, remembering to use her preferred surname, "I hope you are not offended by my next question, because I know you've been through a lot." Jessie hesitated, wondering if it was wise to press his luck with this woman, knowing that his next question, necessary as it was, might push her over the edge. "I'm curious, though, why you never instituted paternity proceedings on your own. After all, in reviewing the files and grant records, here, I see that you have been off of public assistance several times, for some years at a stretch, evidently because of your prior marriages."

"Yeah, a lot of damn good that did for me," Linda Whitman replied. "Those men never did nothin' for me 'cept give me more babies, more troubles and more bruises. No man ever paid me no child support until my last husband, Tony. He maybe sends me a little bit now and then for my youngest boy, Sandy. Never sees the boy very much, though," she added wistfully, looking down at her hands, placed palms down over the paper on her lap. She then drew a deep breath and looked back up, first at her son then at Jessie Jacobs. "You people didn't help things either with all your promises and your delays and doing nothin'," she stated firmly, giving him a scornful glance. The big Anglo, sensing that her patience with him was now about gone, squirmed slightly in his chair, and glanced down again at the open file in front of him.

"Well we both know that Mr. Hathaway is the one who's to blame here, Ms. Whitman," Jessie said, using his deepest prosecutorial baritone. "It doesn't make any difference what has happened, really. Mr. Hathaway hasn't paid anything for years and he should have. And it is the responsibility of our agency to see that he does," Jessie stated self-assuredly. The Indian woman lowered her head, again, as if the list of questions on her lap was her only comfort.

"Well if you do get any support out of the man, how much do I get, then?" she quizzed.

Jessie Jacobs then explained to Linda that the money the agency would extract from Sam's father in the form of child support would actually be a debt owed to the agency which paid the public assistance grant to Linda Whitman in the first place. She, in turn, would receive a fifty dollar "pass-through" payment each month, provided that the agency was able to extract payments from Sam's father.

"That's a hell of a small consolation for me, mister," she scoffed.

"Well, yes, that's true, Ms. Whitman," replied Jessie politely. Fifteen years was a long time. "However, once you go off the public assistance grant, Sam's father will be obliged to pay the child support directly to you. So, really, we're acting on your behalf, here, in establishing the youngster's paternity and obtaining child support for you." Having told her all of these things, Jessie felt satisfied that Linda Pawlik Whitman would now have the good sense to review with him a little bit of her background, her case history, and the names of witnesses who could be subpoenaed to the paternity trial. He had noticed one name which appeared frequently throughout the case file — Doris Wallport. Jessie knew Linda's support group was small.

"Tell me," Jessie asked. "I need to get your case ready, now. Is Doris Wallport still available as a witness for you?"

"She's sittin' right outside in the waitin' room, there," said Linda. Jessie Jacobs wanted to know what Doris Wallport knew about Linda's relationship with Ron Hathaway and if there were any other persons Linda could name as witnesses. "Yes," replied Linda. "Doris Wallport's daughter, Darlene. But she still lives in Pendleton. Has a couple of kids. Could come over for the trial, though, if you gave her 'nough time." Linda explained to Jessie that Doris and several of Doris' friends had known Ron Hathaway. She told him that Ron might have said things about Linda to her friends. Then she paused, looking rather skeptically at Jessie again.

"You know, you should review those notes you have in front of you of that meetin' I told you about seven or eight years ago, Mr. Jacobs. I said all of this stuff then, and it's still true now." Jessie flipped back through the file, paused momentarily, scanning the pages, his head moving from side to side.

"Yeah, sure enough, Ms. Whitman, you're right. It's all right here. I'm sorry. Tell you what, I'll get out some subpoenas, but first I'd like to talk to Doris." Jessie glanced over at the boy in the corner of the room, who was still lethargic, slouched in his chair, evidently asleep. Jessie tried to get his attention. "Yo, Sam, can you do us a favor?" boomed Jessie. Sam jerked awake, as Jessie's deep voice reverberated off the walls. "Appreciate it if you'd go out and have Doris Wallport come in and talk to us, O.K.?" Jessie tried to be solicitous in view of the inconvenience. Sam glanced over at his mother.

"What's goin' on, Mom?" he asked, obviously annoyed at being awakened so unexpectedly.

"Go out and bring Doris in, will ya," directed Linda. As Sam disappeared through the door, Jessie changed the subject, remarking to Linda that she had a good looking youngster who appeared very athletic.

"Yeah, uses his fists at school all the time. Can't get him to do a damn thing 'cept fix my car," she retorted. "Kid's no good in school. Fights all the time. He's already on probation. Have to continue bailin' him out of trouble, with the law and juvenile authorities and things like that," she said disgustedly. "I really don't know how long he's goin' to be with me, Mr. Jacobs. That's why I want to get this thing over with as soon as possible." Linda turned around in her chair, now, glancing through the doorway to see what progress Sam had made. Jessie noticed, for the first time, blotches of bare, reddish skin exposed on the side of her head.

Doris Wallport strolled into the room in front of Sam, her white jacket draped over her right arm. Jessie Jacobs stood to greet her, motioning for her to sit in the vacant seat next to Linda which Sam had refused to occupy. He knew immediately from Doris' quick look at Linda that this lady was Linda Whitman's close friend. He had read things about her — how she had shared Linda's suffering with her for the past two decades. More than that, Doris knew that Ron Hathaway had had sexual relations with Linda. Doris told Jessie how she had talked to Linda about her pregnancy, and she remembered Linda informing her that Ron Hathaway was the father.

"Did Mr. Hathaway ever admit that he was the father to you, Ms. Wallport?" Jessie Jacobs asked.

"Maybe. I'm not sure," she answered. She paused, looking up at the ceiling pensively. "Let's see — yes, I think Ron might have mentioned something to me and my daughter. She was only seven or eight at the time. Her name's Darlene Quirin, now."

"I understand she doesn't live over in this neck of the woods," remarked Jessie. Glancing over at Sam in the corner, he noticed the boy was again getting restless, casting sullen looks at them.

"No, she lives in Pendleton with her husband, but I can call her and let her know she'll have to come over and testify if you want me to," she volunteered.

"Good enough," replied Jessie. "Thank you very much," he said appreciatively, as he made a few more notes and glanced over at Sam. Putting his pencil down, Jessie leaned his huge frame back into the swivelling chair, giving the boy a wide grin which had no discernable effect on the youngster's sullen look.

"Sam, need to ask you a few questions that are important, and, really, only you can give me the answers," the big man told him matter-of-factly. "That O.K. with you?"

"I dunno," the boy remarked with a crooked grin. "I 'spose so. Then can we leave?" mumbled the boy, his grin growing sulky again, like a dark cloud. He glanced at Doris, as if expecting her to agree with his request.

"Sure thing, Sam," replied Jessie with a cheerful grin. "We don't want to keep you here any longer than necessary," he reassured the boy. "But my questions are important, O.K.?"

"O.K. What do ya wanna know?" asked the boy.

"Sam, do you remember when your mom, here, told you about your dad?" Jessie wanted to focus his questions on Sam's earliest recollections of what his mother had told him, whether she had mentioned Ron Hathaway or other men.

"I dunno," the boy responded.

"Sure you do," retorted his mother. "Remember I showed you Ron's picture from my high school annual? Remember that?"

The boy slowly nodded his head. Then a look of recollection crossed his face. "Oh, yeah, when I was real young, Mom showed me a picture of Ron and told me he was my dad. She said he even looks like me."

"Do you think you look like Mr. Hathaway, son?" asked Jessie.

"Guess so." He glanced over at Doris and his mother, again. The boy seemed hesitant. "Whenever Mom shows me his picture, she goes 'He looks just like you.' " He paused thoughtfully. "'Actually the spittin' image,'" Sam quoted his mother, almost triumphantly.

"Well, now," replied Jessie. "Would you like to get to know your dad?"

The boy stared back at the investigator. "I dunno. Guess so," the boy stated with a notable lack of enthusiasm. "Mom's said he's just like all the other men, though. Left us to fend for ourselves." The boy looked down between his legs, the visor of his backwards cap tilted up at the gray ceiling. Then, letting out a big sigh, the boy lifted his head again, returning his attention to Jessie across the room. "Even went down to Hathaway Hardware Store, once," he said. "Had neat sporting goods stuff there. Didn't see him, though. Kind of curious, I guess."

"Was it scary for you, Sam?" Jessie knew the question he posed might be difficult for the youngster to answer.

"I dunno. Guess I thought my dad was part Indian. Mom and Doris, over there, taught me to be proud that I'm Indian. Guess he's Anglo, though," the boy added.

"That's interesting, Sam. Can you tell me a little bit about your Indian heritage, son?"

"Nez Perce tribe," the boy replied with a grin. "That's where my name comes from. Mom's told me what the name 'Whitman' is. Comes from Indian people." The pride in the boy's voice was obvious.

"That's really neat, Sam," said Jessie Jacobs. "You must be really proud that you're Indian. That's a great gift to have, you know." Sensing that he was beginning to capture the boy's interest, Jessie wanted to learn more.

"Yeah, sure," the boy replied rather offhandedly. Samuel Whitman suddenly appeared to be growing sullen again.

"Tell me, Sam, do you have any interests?"

"Dunno. What kind of interests do ya mean?"

Eyeing the boy's five-foot-ten-inch frame sprawled in the chair, Jessie turned to his favorite subject. "Like basketball, maybe?"

"Nah," replied the boy. "Just play some ratball once in a while with my friends." He seemed bored. Jessie wanted to draw the youngster out.

"Your mom tells me you're good with your fists," he said, almost teasingly. Sam looked over at Linda, a puzzled look on his face.

"I told him you like to use your fists a lot," she chuckled. Doris followed suit.

"Oh, then you know how to box?" asked Jessie, posing the question in mock surprise. They all laughed.

"He fights a lot," interjected Doris.

"Good," said the big man optimistically. "Maybe you have a real talent for boxing, son," continued Jessie, sensing he might have an opening with the boy after all. "Ever try out?" he asked.

"Naw," replied the boy, lowering his head.

"Why not?" asked Jessie.

"Guess 'cause I was never interested. I dunno," he replied. Jessie could sense the boy's sullenness about to overtake the conversation.

"Well, Sam, I've met a lot of fellas like you that say they don't know what they're good at. But ya know, I've never met anyone yet who hasn't been good at something. Why, all three of my daughters are good at basketball. They play competitive basketball at that," Jessie proudly announced.

"Really. All your daughters play basketball?" he asked. The fact that young women would have any interest in sports, let alone basketball, seemed to pique Sam's interest, though mildly. After all, it was an activity that never even remotely seemed to interest his two sisters.

"Sure do," Jessie proudly responded. "And you know what I've found?" the big man asked rhetorically, not waiting for an answer.

"Every young man has an interest that he's good at — even you, Sam," asserted Jessie with total confidence. Jessie Jacobs now rose from his own chair, walked around the table and delicately plunked his massive body down on the hard metal chair at the end of the table directly facing Sam. Knowing that he was beginning to catch more of the boy's interest than before, he wanted to see if this bored young man, seemingly detached from all of his mom's adult stuff, might open up. After several attempts at trying to find Sam's favorite activities, Jessie learned that the boy had no real sports or outdoor interests, other than a very peculiar one.

"Always dreamed about owning a big truck," the boy said. Then he paused, glancing both ways, then down at his knees. "And a boat," Sam added softly. "Saw some really neat lookin' boats the time I visited Hathaway Sporting Goods, that one time. You know, the kind you pump up with a pump. Guess they use 'em to go fishin' and do white-water stuff. Always thought that would be kind of exciting, but never got to do it."

"Yeah, the kid really used to like drawing boats," Sam's mother interjected. "First it was horses. Then it was boats." The boy rolled his eyes contemptuously. Jessie could tell that Linda's statement was embarrassing Sam, reminding Jessie that he had once been a child who preferred to be treated as an adult.

"Geez, Sam, I don't know if I'd fit in one of them boats, though," remarked Jessie. The thought of Jessie's gigantic bulk perched inside a small donut of an inflatable boat dancing down a raging whitewater, his huge bearded jowls and flabby arms waving about uncontrollably, brought Samuel Whitman rocking forward with sudden and uproarious laughter — a rollicking kind of laugh which filled the room and made Jessie proud that he had finally opened the boy up. Everyone was laughing, now, too.

"What are your dreams?" he asked him, after the boy settled down. They talked about Sam's wanting to go back to Pendleton, maybe, to visit that place in the Wallowa Valley his mother took him to so long ago where his ancestors used to live. But Samuel Whitman's real ambition, Jessie found out, was to be rich and to own a boat and to go exploring. Sam explained to Jessie that at first he thought he might like to try rodeoing like they did in Pendleton. Like his grandfather Joseph had done. But he had decided, later on, that trucking and lakes and rivers fascinated him more. Little Pawlik told him he liked to go fishing, especially the McKenzie and the Willamette. Fishing and screwing around with his buddies — his "associates" — as he referred to them. And playing hooky from school.

111

The boy finally pressed Jessie for details about his dad, details Jessie knew he could not give. Samuel Little Pawlik Whitman asked the large man difficult questions. He wanted to know what was going to happen now. In addition, did Ron Hathaway have children of his own? If so, did Jessie know what Ron Hathaway's children were like, what his wife was like?

"No," replied Jessie, in his gentle manner, repeatedly trying to brush aside Sam's questions as unobtrusively as possible.

But Sam's mother was not to be deterred. Looking down once again at her piece of white paper, Linda had a few questions of her own.

"Do you or the agency know where Mr. Hathaway is now?" she pointedly asked the huge investigator.

"We think Mr. Hathaway's employed in the Willamette Valley," Jessie replied with a deliberate vagueness. He didn't want Linda, or anyone else for that matter, contacting the Hathaway family. He had seen this happen before with public assistance recipients and knew how much more difficult it could make his job. "We will, of course, track him down through his social security number and the employment division records which we have available to us." Jesse knew, after all, that the paternity establishment methodology of the agency, although painfully cumbersome and slow, was safe and reassuring for most folks. Most mothers wanted little or no contact with the men who had fathered their children.

"Well, even if paternity is established, Mr. Hathaway is obviously a total stranger to Sam," Linda Whitman stated resolutely. "Will you be able to represent us if visitation with his father becomes important?" she asked.

Jessie became suddenly frustrated by the legalities of a system. The law did not allow his agency to take care of details such as visitation and all of the feelings that occurred when children were legally united with their biological fathers. Jessie tried to explain these things to Linda Whitman as calmly and as matter-of-factly as he could. Linda, mouth tight and eyes fixed on her lap, said nothing.

"Why do we even have to have a paternity thing, then?" asked Sam. "Can't Mr. Hathaway just come in and say that he's my dad without goin' through all of this?" The boy's questions, simple and direct, challenged Jessie's tact to the hilt.

"Well, Sam, we're probably going to need witnesses and a trial because Mr. Hathaway may deny the fact that, biologically, he is your father." The boy's whole body tensed. "If he does this, then we will have blood drawn from your mother, from your arm and from Mr.

Hathaway to confirm whether or not his blood matches yours." The boy's stunned look changed instantly. His eyes narrowed, producing a sullen, angry cloud.

"Nobody goes and takes my blood unless'n I say so," the boy stated defiantly. Jessie knew that the boy obviously had missed the point and was growing defensive.

"Sam, because your father may not think he's your father after all these years, that gives him a legal right to request that blood tests be performed," the large man stated as reassuringly as he could. "Actually it's no big deal, they just prick your arm with a needle and take a little blood, is all," he added as nonchalantly as he could. Jessie had no further answer for the young man, except to say that some day Sam's dad would, perhaps, sit down to talk about these things in his own way. After all, Mr. Hathaway had children of his own, Jessie explained.

"I wish he would'a done that a long time ago," the boy replied. There was an awkward silence. Jessie Jacobs felt a deep aching pain in his gut. Things should have been done far sooner by the agency. This woman and her son deserved that. He would assure them that there would be no more delays.

"Sam, as long as I'm involved in this with you and your mom, everything is going to be O.K." the large man said. Sam stared back at him with a distrustful look Jessie had not seen before, the boy's eyes darkening so suddenly that Jessie was taken aback.

"How do you know that?" snapped Sam. "Ya don't even know me, or my mom," he threw at him. "How do you know everything's gonna be O.K.?"

"Yeah," replied Linda. "Who are you, anyway! Don't feed us that line of crap, Mr. Jacobs. You don't really know if things will be all right." Jessie, looking at the boy's face, reddened now, sensing that the boy felt betrayed by him because of his mother's sense of indignation.

"Fuck this, anyway!" Sam blurted out with venom. "I juss wanna get the hell outta here!" The boy leaped to his feet, turning his back on Jessie Jacobs, and stormed out of the room.

"Oh, Christ," groaned Linda. "Doris, will you please go out and calm him down. Stay out there, will ya. See that he don't mess things up. I'll only be a few more minutes, O.K.?" she implored.

"Sure, honey," replied Doris Wallport. "Take as long as you like. I'll talk to Sam, you know. Everything will be fine," Doris Wallport said with a quiet, reassuring tone. She got up to leave, putting on her white coat, turning as she left to offer Jessie a last apologetic glance.

"Ms. Whitman, I'm really sorry for all that," Jessie said, trying to calm an obviously distressed woman who seemed anxious to leave.

"We'll schedule the DNA blood tests as soon as we are able to notify Mr. Hathaway. I hope he doesn't deny that he's the father." Linda Whitman seemed not to care what the big man had to offer.

"The boy's on juvenile probation, ya know," she said bitterly, glowering at the files as Jessie walked back to his seat across the table from her. "Sam's barely in the ninth grade. Had to hold him back a year. Has no interest in school 'cept girls and his no good doper friends. All of his friends are troublemakers at school. I have all I can do just to take care of his younger brother. I can't nursemaid Sam no more," she stated flatly.

"Well, the boy doesn't seem all that bad," Jessie replied in his usual bighearted way.

"Yeah. I guess he needed a father a long time ago," she replied softly. "To show him things, to teach him things. I haven't been able to do that." She paused now, and sat silent for a long time, looking down at her paper. "Has been responsible enough to babysit his little half brother, Sandy, when I had to work," she continued. "He loves his little brother. He loves to fix things, too. Has kept my car runnin' longer than I'd ever hoped," she chuckled. "Won't do anything else I tell him, though," she stated with a fatalism that caused her shoulders to sag.

"Listen, Ms. Whitman, if Sam messes up, just give me a call," he said, looking directly at her. "I do a lot of counseling with runaways, and I really like kids. I promise you, I'll try and help out." He dropped his glance now, his eyes searching for his front shirt pocket beneath his left suspender strap. His massive right hand reached in and grabbed a card which he held out to her. "Here, here's my card. If somethin' happens, give me a call, O.K.?" Linda nodded.

"Can we go, now?" she asked. "I have a doctor's appointment. Doctor wants me there by 5:00."

"Sure thing, Ms. Whitman," said Jessie. "I want to make things as easy for you as I can," he added.

"Good," replied Linda Whitman. "Because I have some health problems. Which is another reason why I want things to go smoothly." Jessie was puzzled. He asked her, briefly, to describe her health problems. The Indian woman said she did not want to, and hadn't mentioned this before, especially in front of her boy and her best friend. Reaching around behind him from his chair, which now squeaked and groaned painfully again, Jessie lifted a form out of one of the twenty or so slots from a form box hanging on the wall behind him. Placing the form on the table in front of Linda Whitman, he handed her his pen which he extracted from the same front pocket of his flannel shirt. "I'll need you to sign this authorization for me, Ms. Whitman, so that I can get your medical records."

"Why do you need my medical records?" she asked, looking perplexed. Jessie explained to her that he would need an updated medical authorization form to provide information to the agency concerning the events and circumstances surrounding Samuel's birth as well as any relevant medical history which the agency might be required to produce. He explained that Sam's father might hire a lawyer and his lawyer might happen to ask for this information. The court, most certainly, would require the agency to provide her medical records. Linda seemed disconcerted at the prospect that a man she had not seen for fifteen years could violate her privacy so easily.

"Well, Mr. Jacobs, thank you for your patience," Sam's mother finally stated in a dignified tone. She seemed strangely reconciled to herself. Beneath all the suffering this woman had faced, something from within her evinced a pride which Jessie Jacobs admired. They shook hands. He nodded at her and she turned, walking the few steps out through the door. He returned to his swivel chair, hearing it squeak as he sat down and wondered what her medical history contained. What had seemed to be a routine question had gone strangely unanswered.

Jessie Jacobs had finished a long, tiring day, not the least of which was meeting a proud woman with secrets she did not wish to share with him, and about which he couldn't stop wondering. And he had met a proud but angry young man.

Like so many young men who had passed through his life before, Samuel Whitman seemed to want to share something with him, but didn't quite know how. He knew it was perhaps because the youngster had never had a teacher who had taught him things about his own emotions and feelings, how to handle his fears, things that had seemed obvious to Jessie Jacobs but which weren't obvious at all to Samuel Whitman.

In the back of his mind, Jessie Jacobs worried that perhaps he might be privy to an unavoidable tragedy occurring in young Samuel Whitman's life that not even he, nor anyone else, could prevent.

Getting up slowly from his chair, he felt the soreness in his back and legs return again as his body adjusted. He strode over to the curtainless, metal-framed sliding window of the little inner office he had occupied all day long, rubbing his eyes with his massive fists. He peered out at the April rain which continued to pour. The rain had drenched everything that day. He noticed how the water cascaded off the roof to his right, part of the gutter having been broken and missing for quite some time. He watched as the rainwater rolled and slid off the end of the broken gutter and fell like a waterfall, splashing dirt and mud on the corner of the building, forming an impact crater filled with grimy, brownish residue about the size of the small table he'd labored on since early that morning.

CHAPTER 13

A CAPSIZE

Above the Friday evening din of jukebox music, the chatter of patrons, clatter of beer glasses and the spreading clouds of cigarette smoke at The Keg, Ron Hathaway had been commiserating with three of his drinking buddies from work. They were all hunkered down around a table in the back — Monte DeMarco, the newlywed, Larry Craig, the sports jock, and a fellow journeyman carpenter — the framer who had replaced Randy Baccus — named Jeff Claymore. Late into the evening, in between frequent pitchers of beer, Ron's problems at work and his paternity case had by now become totally threadworn and maudlin.

"Shit, Ron, why don't you stop jabbering and just go give Linda a call right now," Larry finally suggested.

"You've been talking about her all night long," observed Monte.

"What's the matter?" chimed in Jeff, the new framer. "Don't ya have any balls, man? Give the woman a call, for chrissakes, and stop talking about her."

Ron heard the voices coming in at him and didn't know what to do. He felt the quarters in his pocket, slowly turning them in his left hand the whole evening. He sat there at the table with his drinking buddies, eyes fixed glumly on the pitcher of beer sitting in the center of the table.

"What the hell, I've already screwed things up enough already. Job at Dahlberg's in the toilet. Don't have anything else to lose. I'll just give her a call. I won't say anything I'm not s'posed to." Ron felt the same sensation he'd experienced in the war. A tightness in his gut. Throbbing temples. Sweat clinging to his forehead and chilling the back of his neck.

He got up slowly from the table, his shattered left leg still bothering him on this cold winter evening. He noticed the same weakness in his legs and shakiness in his hands he'd felt on sweeps in the war. The dizziness hit him. The booze, though, had numbed his leg and mind enough to allow him to walk painlessly the twenty feet over to the jukebox. Leaning on the machine with his outstretched right arm, he withdrew one of his quarters and dropped it in. As if sensing that he needed something comforting to accompany him to the phone booth, he selected a Waylon Jennings tune.

Turning, he ambled slowly to the pay phone, fumbling for another quarter with his left hand. The phone rested on the smudged, dingy yellow wall next to the restroom in the hallway behind the bar. The jukebox began playing the lilting country western melody from his favorite unpredictable singer. Standing next to the phone booth, he stared at the wall, the music barely audible as it drifted lazily back his way. He felt the vertigo effect from the booze move through his head in dizzying surges and swells, making his eyes bounce, the phone booth bob. The wall, the hallway, started to slowly turn. Gripping the phone booth, he took out his quarter, placing it at the mouth of the slot. He closed his eyes. The spinning seemed to slow momentarily. He dropped the quarter in and picked up the receiver.

"Christ a-mighty, what the hell am I gonna say?" he muttered. "This is nuts." He hesitated. "Oh Christ!" He punched out the seven numbers. The phone rang for what seemed like five minutes. The spinning started once more. The hot rush of adrenaline now began to pound at his temples. He felt his heart beat faster. The ringing stopped. He closed his eyes again.

"Hello, hello?" came the tired, distant female voice at the other end.

* * * * *

Ron lifted his head from the lines of the oak table, seeing the shape of the telephone receiver now mutate itself into the bottle cap on the table in front of him. He remembered he was at home now.

A biting cold February wind, blowing through the Willamette Valley, rattled the screen door. Only the dimmer glass-belled piano light remained on in the living room. All else was quiet. Ron sat with his right arm cocked sideways, hands gripping a quart of his favorite stout malt liquor. His Caterpillar hat was perched atop the open end of the quart bottle. Stooped shoulders framed Ron's bloodshot eyes, fixed on the center of the table ahead. Tracing a road map for the upturned bottle cap in the center of the table, his head weaved as it seemed to follow the golden cap along the interlacing strains of the oak table. His mouth was slack, as if numbed.

Melissa Hathaway sat across the oak kitchen table from her husband, her left hand encircling a freshly brewed cup of coffee. Leaning back in the high wooden chair, she reached over and set the half-empty pot of coffee on the front burner of the white gas stove.

Melissa was hot with anger and frustration. She had just put a restless Josh down to sleep with his favorite animal story. Trying to contain her anger, she stared across at her husband.

"Ron, we can't go on like this," she said in a fierce whisper. Her husband's bloodshot eyes were fixed on her. He was silent.

"What's to say?" he shrugged. He looked down again at the table, trying to avert her direct gaze.

"Ron," she implored. "You promised you'd be home right after work so we could talk. The situation and all, especially with your not being able to drive all the time — we've got to figure this out! You know you've got those restrictions on your driving. Why do you do this?" She struggled to hold herself back.

"I know. I was gonna come right home, hon." He let the words slip out slowly, feeling a deep boozy sadness.

"You know your drinking is affecting the boys, Ron. You come home drunk and act funny. Rob has been staying up in his room and won't come down. He is frightened to death of you." She spoke evenly and with conviction. She tried to make eye contact with him but couldn't quite draw his attention.

"Do you have any idea what effect your drinking's had on Josh?" She raised her voice now. "Any inkling at all?" Ron turned his head away. "Ron, I'm never home now when he needs me for school work. He's fallen behind. His special education teacher has called me." She withdrew from him for a second, then resumed. "Josh came to me the other day and whispered something to me, Ron — one of his little secrets I'm supposed to not tell. Want to know what he said?" she asked, moving her head to the left, trying to catch Ron's sideways glance at her. "'Why doesn't Daddy seem like Daddy anymore, Mom? Is Daddy sick? Does Daddy still love me, Mom?' — That's what he said, Ron." Her husband's mouth fell open, eyes glistening.

"Jesus, 'Lissa, we've been going through a hell of an ordeal, here." Ron was trying to sound sympathetic.

"No, Ron. The boys and I have been going through a hell of an ordeal. You're out feeling sorry for yourself, spending our money getting drunk! Your drinking is costing us a fortune. Do you know how much money your drinking is costing every week? Do you have any idea? Do you really care?" The rapid fire of her anger was intimidating.

"You know I love you," he added plaintively, trying to touch her softer side.

"Then why the hell were you out so late, drinking again, goddamn it?!" she shot back. "You absolutely know that your job, our livelihood, is at stake here," she added, her hands outstretched.

"Shit, I dunno, I just felt like it, I guess," Ron retorted defensively.

"Just felt like it? Why don't you think of me and the kids, at least your kids?"

"Christ, woman — that's all I can think about is my kids," he blurted. "And Samuel," he said quietly, his voice almost a cry. "I've been so torn. I finally decided to call Linda tonight." He was weeping. "Jesus, I didn't think I could ever do it."

"What did she say, Ron?" Melissa asked earnestly, her eyes now wide and fixed on him. "Is that what's bothering you? What did she say? What did she tell you? What things did you talk about? What did you say?" Melissa was hoping that her husband, for once, might have done the right thing by talking to the woman.

"Oh, Christ, I was pretty drunk. Her voice sounded pretty strange. I really can't remember...," his voice trailed off.

Melissa's eyes darkened, her mouth sank.

"Listen to me, Ron. We've been through this before with your drinking. You've got to get a grip, man," she said with conviction.

"Get a grip, 'Lissa? Christ almighty." Ron took another high, arching swig of malt liquor from the quart bottle mouth. His Caterpillar hat now rested on the oak kitchen table. As his chin and head descended from a long swallow, he instinctively pushed the bottle out to the center of the table, as if offering Melissa a drink. Head bowed, he was thinking to himself. Got to tell her what's happened at work.

She caught a whiff of the bitter hops from his breath. Now utterly consumed with disgust, she grabbed the quart bottle and whirled around, all in one blurred motion, throwing the bottle and its contents into the kitchen sink. "Bam," the bottle struck the metallic sink. For a split second, Ron heard his nine-foot oar break — "Bang." Ron felt himself losing control, the room starting to turn sideways.

"Your goddamn drinking is to blame for all of this!" she hurled back at him. "You son-of-a-bitch, you're screwing me and the kids just like you screwed whats-her-name, Linda!" Her face was aflame, eyes burning into him. With a burst of venom, she had flung her thunderbolt across at his now shrunken, withdrawn form in the chair.

Ron felt the hard paddle of Linda's name strike the side of his head. Glancing upwards, for an instant he saw her hands and teeth clenched with rage as the room started to swirl.

He would not dare tell her now that he had lost his job at Dahlberg.

He saw Melissa's deep, penetrating eyes blazing at the center of the drunken whirlpool. His mind flipped backwards.

His oar broken, his boat was now caught helplessly careening in the crosscurrent of a murderous twenty-foot-high Grand Canyon Lava Rapids thunder roller. He felt his 400-pound inflatable boat tossed skyward by the jagged roller coaster waves like a spiraling leaf spinning up in a gust of wind. He was thrown clear of the sturdy craft like a rag doll. Amidst the crashing water and disorienting spray, his face and hands seemed to float in a quiet space for a split second, then crashed down into the cold crush of the whitewater rapids. He felt his legs and arms furiously whipped about like spaghetti. He was in a total panic. He knew not who or where he was. Finally, he was beneath the thundering water and an eerie silence ensued. The cold had a strange and deadening effect, an eerie calmness. He struggled to comprehend what had happened.

His trip in the "Tiger Tub" had disintegrated in a split second. He saw the overturned craft from beneath, dodging helplessly down the waterway, equipment still lashed to the underside, loose ends — tackle, coolers, debris of all kinds — bobbing aimlessly alongside. Now he discovered that his once loosely tied life jacket had been ripped from his body. The mindless, relentlessly numbing current pushed him cruelly down and under. His eyes blinked upwards at the disappearing overturned boat. He lay like a pile-driven patch of moss on a battered boulder somewhere beneath the raging current. He knew that his last breath of air would be gone in seconds. He must either break out, now, or he would die.

"What the hell do you expect me to do, 'Lissa, for chrissakes?" The words came out haltingly. "Do you want me to raise this kid? Shit, I'm just barely able to support us, let alone pay all of this goddamn child support for a little delinquent bastard." He groped for the anger which he knew would help him survive. "Don't you get it, woman? We're total strangers to each other." He paused, again, to catch his breath. "Samuel Whitman. That's his name on those damn papers," he snapped. "Christ, the kid doesn't even have my last name! Why should I pay any support for this kid?"

He slowly got up from the table, tripping and swaying over to the refrigerator. His sweaty, dark hair askew, he glanced around nervously for that extra beer he thought he had secretly stashed.

"I got rid of your late night 'coup de grace' too," she remarked sarcastically.

Ron, drunk and bewildered, tried to summon his anger but couldn't. He crumbled down next to the refrigerator. He looked up at her through the milky haze with bloodshot eyes. He felt the squeezing, suffocating weight next to that boulder under the thunderous river.

Awash in the dense, boozy fog of his blurry and random thoughts came Linda's tired, distant voice. But what the hell was it that she had said? Ron's mind struggled for a foothold.

He clenched his teeth, his head and shoulders flattened against the refrigerator, beneath the onslaught. He glared stupidly at the dirty linoleum cracks on the floor next to the refrigerator. His thoughts of the angry current — being pinned by the relentless pressure of it all — brought on a tightness in his chest which he had never felt before.

Then his mind, in a drunken spasm of self-survival, pulled him, struggling against the current of the booze, to his feet. Got to survive, he thought wildly to himself. Can't suffocate and drown. This is all so fucking senseless! He expelled a gasp of air, as he felt the sting of Melissa's look strike right into his beating heart.

"I've got to get the hell outta here," he blurted out. Melissa, hysterical now, jumped up from the table to grab him. "Where are you going?" she cried out, as he brushed her aside and bolted out the kitchen door into the cold winter night. She ran to the banging screen door, cursing him, weeping. She stood there, framed in the doorway against the cold night.

CHAPTER 14

AT THE CONFLUENCE

The stinging twenty degree cold reached through the open window of the cab like a pair of bony icicle hands, clawing at Ron Hathaway's face, and waking him from his drunken stupor. The feeling was actually comforting to Ron, now, as the burn from his confrontation with Melissa began to subside. He felt at home and safe, again, in his rig driving through the blackened streets of Springfield.

Taking a left turn with his pickup, he drove back towards The Keg.

Worrying for half a second that he might have forgotten his wallet, along with his watch, he reached behind to check his rear pocket and noticed the familiar bulge, only to remember that he was driving on a restricted license, and that this hour was far outside the work-time restrictions that had been placed upon him. Restrictions that were meaningless now because he was out of a job. Ron eased his foot off the gas pedal.

The wintry hands encircling his face continued to massage away the dense fog that had enshrouded him earlier at The Keg and his brief telephone conversation with Linda. Her tired voice on the phone, her tone of recognition and then her hesitancy, knowing that he'd been drinking, came back. The woman had probably been in no mood to casually discuss Sam's existence after fifteen years. But he couldn't quite remember. How stupid, he thought. Somehow Sam had been mentioned. There had been a long, final silence and then Linda had said something. "He needs his father, Ron."

"I'll call you back," he had told her. He wondered why he had blurted that out.

Ron glanced over to his left and saw that Landon Saxton had left the neon sign on. The garish red letters told him that it wasn't quite 2:00 in the morning — closing time. He jockeyed his pickup through the potholes and puddles of the parking lot, nestling his rig next to the side of his favorite watering hole. Glancing around, he noticed a taxi cab which had just rolled up to the front entrance.

Ron turned off the ignition and breathed in, comforted by the sense of his being in familiar surroundings. He was also relieved at having seen no patrol cars.

Opening the door to the bar, his eyes squinted as the lights from inside, which were turned completely on, seemed to glare down at him. Glancing over at Landon, who gave him a friendly "hello," Ron knew that the bar would be shut down any minute.

The fifty-five-year-old barkeep looked tired. His brown eyes were set back in dark circles beneath his long, grayish, swept back hair. Shoulders slightly stooped, and armpits darkened with the sweat of a fourteen hour shift, he was serving up coffee to two men seated at the bar.

Near the front entrance, an elderly grizzled man, obviously having difficulty with balance and speech, was seated in a chair and mumbling some complaints to the taxi driver. "Old Bill" they called him, was trying to gesture with his hands. Sensing that the discussion was taking too long, Landon interceded, telling the driver to "go ahead and take Bill home and put it on my tab, O.K.?" Ron smiled, knowing that Landon would always call a cab for old Bill when he had too much to drink. "Insurance" — that's what Landon had called it. Better to spend ten or fifteen dollars on a cab for an annoyed patron than to get shut down.

"Hey, Landon, got time to serve one last brew tonight?" Ron asked anxiously. Landon Saxton's look of apprehension and his glance at the clock told Ron that the barkeep was ready to leave.

"Sorry, Ron, can't accommodate you tonight," Landon said. "Can I get you a cup of coffee?" For a moment Ron was crushed. Still, the idea of a hot cup of coffee right now seemed inviting to Ron as he stood at the bar, both elbows resting for support. He nudged over and sat on the gray stool across from Landon.

"Yeah, that sounds good," said Ron. "Might help me sober up," he added, as he glanced over at old Bill being escorted out the front door, muttering slurred obscenities as the taxi driver led him away. "How long you gonna be stayin', Landon?"

"'Bout fifteen more minutes. Why? Do you need somethin'?"

Ron paused. "Yeah, I just wanted to know if it would be O.K. to make a phone call. I'll keep it short, O.K.?"

"Sounds good to me. I'll just come back and holler at ya when I get ready to leave," the barkeep winked as he handed Ron a white mug full of steaming black coffee.

Ron walked slowly over to the phone booth in the back of The Keg for the second time that night. He took a couple of sips from the mug, setting it down on the table next to the phone booth. The melody from Waylon Jennings' song earlier that night played again in his mind. From his cache in his left pocket he removed a quarter, plunked it in and dialed Linda's number. The phone rang and rang. As he waited, Ron realized that Linda might be more than a little annoyed at his second intrusion at such a late hour.

"Hello," came a sleepy female voice. The voice was unfamiliar to Ron.

"Hi, this is Ron again," he said tentatively. "Linda?" he asked even more tentatively.

"No, this is Susan," said the voice rather briskly. "You wanta speak to my mom?"

"Yes, if it's O.K. If she's not asleep."

"I'll go get her." The girl sounded irritated. Ron listened intently, hearing a door open and whispered, anxious conversation. The wait was longer than it should have been. He worried that his impulsive call might have angered Linda. He thought of suddenly hanging up but caught himself, remembering that he had blurted out his first name to the young woman, Susan.

"Hello, again, stranger," came Linda's slow, tired voice over the phone. "Man, you sure keep late trucker's hours," she said half jokingly. "Actually, can't get no sleep tonight. Insomnia, I guess."

Ron felt relieved. For an instant, he tried to place Linda's voice with the woman he had remembered from his distant past.

"Yeah, I kind of needed to call you back, Linda," he said. "Needed to sober up some. Sorry about that first call," he apologized. "Guess I just wanted to see how you are, how you're doin', Linda." Then Ron thought of Sam, but decided to say nothing. "Heard you were in the Eugene area and thought I'd touch bases for old time's sake. How 'bout it?" Ron sensed that perhaps Linda would know that his out-of-place call at 2:00 in the morning was not simply a casual get acquainted gesture.

"Well, Ron, it's been a long time. Been through a lot of changes, ya know." There was a deliberate pause. "You and I both know what's goin' on here," she added, rather dryly. Ron felt his heart beat faster, the dizzying effect of the booze falling off like a dry blanket.

"Well, yeah, I've been served with papers from the state, ya know," he retorted. "The thing's kind of put me and my family through some changes, too," he slowly explained. The conversation seemed unreal. Still, Ron hoped that his direct approach — although mistimed — might relax the woman enough to allow them to get acquainted again. "How 'bout tonight, Linda?" Ron asked, half expecting Linda to either slam the receiver down or curse at him, or both.

"Well, you haven't changed much, Hathaway. Remember you always liked to call me in the middle of the night?" she asked. "Always wantin' to party." The thought, the image, of what he had been suddenly struck Ron fully now. The nights after bar hopping in Pendleton when he would party, constantly phoning Linda at odd hours in the morning. She seemed so full of energy then. So approachable. He remembered her long, coal black hair. Quite an attractive young woman. He remembered her brown skin, those beautiful dark eyes perched atop her high cheek bones, her full lips and even fuller breasts.

"Yeah, those were the days," he quietly reminisced.

"Well, I've slowed down quite a bit, Ron, over the years," she offered. "Havin' kids will do that to you, ya know." Linda's flat, unemotional voice evaporated the image of the younger woman.

"Well, yeah, Linda, I got your address and phone number through the paternity case but I didn't wanna just call you up and come over and barge in." Ron paused, deliberating, wanting the woman to appreciate that he respected her privacy. "Would it be O.K. if I come over for a little bit?"

"Yeah, I guess," she said. "Are you sure you know where I'm stayin'?" she asked.

"Well, I've had your address for some time now and I'm calling you from The Keg over here in Springfield. I think I can get there in about twenty minutes or maybe a half-hour at the outside," said Ron. "Is that O.K. with you?"

"Yeah, its an apartment ya know and we're in number seven on the bottom floor," she offered. "Be sure and park out in the street, 'cause at this hour I don't think there'll be any parkin' spaces available outside."

"O.K., we'll see you then," he said, hearing her say "bye." He slowly put the receiver down and paused for a minute, going over the conversation again in his head. Seeing his mug on the table, he reached over and raised it to his lips. He slowly sipped the hot coffee, feeling it warm his throat.

Thoughts of Linda Whitman and his long-ago friends, "the Raunches" back in Pendleton, reminded him that she had always been a good lay. So wild. He felt the rough bed sheets and naked touches, but did not quite remember, very often, the sexual release.

Still, he had experienced an arousal for Linda, despite his lack of feeling which he so desperately drowned in booze. The press of Linda's breasts and her special touching of him — her mouth and tongue — had awakened a lustful yearning within him.

But Linda hadn't been the only one. Rhonda, a pretty full-figured girl with lips which were so big and soft — softer and more sensuous than Linda's — had a passion for using her mouth. Brenda, a tougher older girl, smoked and drank a lot. He remembered her references to sex as "bed games." One plump, rather dowdy girl, nicknamed Babs, was Linda's closest friend. He remembered that this girl was more standoffish than the rest.

Then there was Carol, a long-legged blond girl with such a well shaped rear end that Ron's heart raced, even now, as visions of his escapades with her entered his head. When he had come out to Portland, he had even talked about Carol to his friend Don Karr and remembered how Don jokingly made that unusual reference to her derriere, concocted from his penchant for Greco-Roman history. Laughing, Don explained to his younger friend that everyone thought Carol was "a very callipygian woman."

Later he actually looked up the fancy word — it meant having a well-shaped buttocks — and wrote it on a piece of paper which he stuck in his wallet.

The thought made him slowly shake his head as the lights over the pool tables were suddenly shut off. It was Linda, only Linda, who seemed to understand what he had been through as a "leg" — an infantryman — in the war. Perhaps Linda's own suffering...

Then, as Ron Hathaway stood there, he remembered. The only person who had really relived the ambush with him. The death. About his best friend Leo's eyes. He had been drunk that one night with Linda Whitman at her place. Linda knew it all.

"Leo the Lerp." In Nam, they called a Long Range Reconnaissance Patrol a LRRP, or Lerp, for short. And that's what they called his best friend Leopold. The name fit, he had told her. He was from a large Hispanic family. He had known a hard life, streetwise, a tough kid who grew up in a gang-infested neighborhood in south L.A. He sported an uproarious sense of humor from the streets. Leo was always playing cards and cutting the air with banter which seemed to ease the tension between patrols, tension which constantly hung in the air like a lingering mist.

Ron was supposed to walk point for the patrol that sunlit morning of May 16, 1968, but Leo took his place. Seems a poker game the night before decided the issue. Not quite like Russian roulette.

The banter was casual, almost unreal, during that morning's aborted patrol. "Hey Halfway," exclaimed Leo — that's the name his buddy had given Ron. "Gotta duke?"

"Sure thing, Lerp" Ron replied, reaching for the pack of half-empty smokes he carried just above his ammo belt. The morning air was quiet but tense. Leo, Ron and five others had plodded along from dike to dike, in the sweltering heat, sweating in the mud-filled rice paddies, stopping for short breaks to rest and light up the smokes most of them stowed in their helmet liners. It always seemed to Ron that Leo ran out of smokes first. "Just remember you owe me," added Ron, approaching Leo from behind as his friend started to lift himself up onto the grass dike just ahead. A small dirt road ran lengthwise along the dike into a treeline off to the right.

"Thug...thug...thug!" came the sound of mortars.

"Incoming!" screamed Leo.

"Get on the goddamned radio!" Ron yelled out to the radio man behind him, still struggling through the muck. Earth rattling explosions heaved dirt, vegetation and water in all directions amidst the clatter of machine gun fire. Instinctively, Ron dropped and buried his whole body into the muck, looking up just once, seeing Leo glance back at him from the top of the dike. Then the whole ground around him rose up, churned and fell, as if some giant pulverizer passed over all of them, a screaming, flaming juggernaut. Then it stopped.

Ron lay there a long time, paralyzed, unable to even lift his head. Finally, he heard the whirlwind pounding of the gun ship propellers overhead and the thunderous staccato of their covering fire blazing deadly metal down on those in the treeline who had caught the patrol unawares.

Only then did Ron inhale deeply and crawl up to where he had last seen his buddy.

Leo lay on his back, his right arm completely severed about an inch or two below the shoulder. Leo's left boot was missing, having been blown off by the concussion from the mortars. What was left of his midsection lay open, its contents spewed on his pants and the ground.

Ron sat down next to his buddy and cried. Others came by later, but Ron lost all track of them. Despite his own injury, or maybe because of it, he even lost track of himself. His left knee had been split open and broken with shrapnel from a mortar round, exposing pieces of his dark tibia. All he could remember was his best friend's last words — a simple request for a smoke. And Ron's last words to him — "remember you owe me."

All he could see were Leo's eyes.

Only Linda Whitman knew the blood and torn human flesh of his best friend dying. Only she knew anything of the demons which would cause him to look backwards for the rest of his life.

* * * * *

As Ron left the reassuring confines of The Keg Tavern, saying a "good evening" and "thanks" to Landon, Ron wondered if he would meet the same girl he had known then. Quietly, carefully, he glanced around and backed his ancient pickup through the potholes and mud-puddles of the parking lot.

Suddenly a patrol car confronted him, proceeding slowly past The Keg. The patrol car braked. Ron waited.

The patrol car turned off into the parking lot, cruising slowly in the opposite direction, its headlights off. Ron pulled his rig up to the front of the tavern. He turned off the ignition. His grip on the wheel froze as he caught the vacant overheads of the white-topped patrol car in his rearview mirror. It had crept up not fifty feet behind and was stopped. The chrome door-mounted searchlight pointed menacingly at him, even though turned off. In an instant, Ron's head pounded out his drunk driving arrest in Eugene. The cold cement floor of the jail reached up through to his face. No license. No job. No meeting with Linda and Sam. Ron felt his heart pound under his shirt as he waited for the cop to confront him.

The sharp wowing of the siren pierced through, jolting Ron upright, the overheads instantly bathing him in a kaleidoscope of blue and red swirling flashes. The black-and-white roared past, Ron barely glimpsing the officer intently hunched over the wheel. The car weaved out of the lot, turning and accelerating with a sharp, squealing screech up the road — apparently responding to an urgent call.

Ron's knuckle-white grip on the wheel slowly released. He inhaled what seemed like his first long, full breath of the evening. The coolness in his nostrils entered his tense chest and eased him back to a steady breathing. Slowly, timidly getting out of his rig, he poked his head inside The Keg.

"Hey, Landon, can I take the rest of that black coffee from you tonight?" he asked. He had caught Landon on his way out. Turning, Landon glanced at the coffee pot, still about half full but turned off.

"Gonna cost you an arm and a leg, fella," Landon laughed. "That cop's been out here every night, now, for the past week," he added, slowly shaking his head.

"Scared the shit outta me."

Filling the stained, cracked red mug Ron had retrieved from his rig, Landon turned back and remarked, "Gimme a buck next time you come in, O.K.?"

"Sure thing. Hey, thanks again, buddy. Insurance, ya know." The barkeep smiled. Ron nudged his rig forward, feeling the old pickup jar and jostle through the obstacle course Landon called his parking lot. Ron carefully peered up the dark, vacant roadway for the patrol car.

Thirty-five minutes later, Ron pulled his truck up alongside a row of apartment houses on Twelfth Street on the outskirts of Eugene. Situated off of the main boulevard in a treeless location, the two-story apartment building was surrounded by white-lined asphalt parking spaces and cement walkways. The wood-paneled building was stained an ugly brown, which appeared even dirtier in the reflection of the garish street lights.

The cold air was less comforting, now. Ron began to shiver uncomfortably, realizing that he was about to meet a youngster — perhaps his son — he had not even seen since his birth. And he would see Samuel's mother again, the Indian girl he had befriended so long ago, hoping that, somehow, she had not changed.

Moving along the bottom row of apartments, he saw the number "7" stenciled on the front door. There was no porch light on. Walking up and peering around the open curtains, he saw a light through the front window in the back. He knocked softly. He waited. The door opened with a squeak, catching on the chain bolt. A young girl's face appeared through the open space between the door frame and the bolted door.

"Hi, I'm Susan." She was rubbing her eyes. "You must be Ron," came the young girl's tired voice. For an instant, Ron stared at her. She still had the long dark flowing hair and the beautiful black eyes resting on high brown-skinned cheekbones. Those full lips. The young girl looked just like Linda. Ron was startled.

"You look just like your mom," Ron remarked. The young girl stared back at him, a puzzled look on her face. The door closed suddenly in Ron's face. He heard the chain bolt sliding. As the door slowly crept open, the young girl, wearing a bright pink bathrobe, stood in the small living room looking intently at him. Behind her, an older woman was draped in a white bathrobe.

Glancing past the young girl, Ron recognized Linda, her arms folded across her chest, standing there with a tired grin. There were still those same dark eyes set above the high cheekbones. But the nose. Ron noticed a crookedness to her nose. Linda's long, beautiful black hair was gone. Her hair was shorter, now, pulled back tightly. And Linda had put on much weight.

"Well you're a sorry sight, standin' there at 2:30 in the mornin'," said the Indian woman. "You look like an escaped war criminal," she joked with that same old casualness that now came back to Ron from those days long ago.

"My God, Linda, you've changed," exclaimed Ron. "Fifteen years. My God!" he repeated, and wondered, too late, whether he had hurt her.

"Well, I couldn't have fallen apart that badly," she chided him. Ron laughed nervously. Linda's daughter, having closed the front door behind Ron, now seated herself at the kitchen table, just off the living room.

"Oh, I'm sorry, Linda. I didn't mean it like that," offered Ron. "I'm just so surprised. It's so strange to see you again after fifteen years." He paused. "Your daughter over there looks just exactly like I remembered you, Linda." Susan glanced over at her mother, trying to understand the significance of what this strange man was saying.

"Now that's the compliment I was waitin' to hear from you," laughed Linda. "Let's sit down," she said, motioning to the frayed, dark green living room couch, resting opposite a large, slightly more tattered green and white cloth chair.

Linda Pawlik walked slowly and deliberately, easing herself into the worn chair. As she turned to address Susan, telling her that she was O.K. and that Susan could go back to bed, Ron noticed, again, that her hair had thinned considerably over the years. Patches of hair had fallen out. Her sallow complexion exhibited a sickly jaundice in places — altogether different from the rich brownish bronze skin tone he remembered. But what was more remarkable was Linda's face, how it sagged, changed from its former youthful appearance, from the full lips and more ripened appearance to a kind of ashen, puffy pallor. Her lips were pursed and cracked. A peculiar sort of sunken darkness to her eyes conveyed a profound, almost deathly, tiredness. She seemed weak, steadying herself as she sank into the old chair across from him.

"You look tired, Ron," she observed. She appeared to Ron to be on the brink of collapsing herself. Her remarks seemed ridiculously out of place.

"Well, yeah, it's been kind of rough, as I told you. I'm just glad you let me come over. I've really thought about this a lot," he went on.

"How do you mean?"

"Well, it was a real big blow to learn that I had been listed as Sam's father, ya know. Just couldn't get used to it, I guess," the words tumbled out. Linda looked at him intently. He half expected her to say something sarcastic. "I never knew about the boy until I got this letter from the state that I told you about." Linda waved him off with her left hand and a half-amused look on her face.

"Come on, darlin', you remember when I was pregnant. Me telling you I was pregnant." Her dark-set eyes, full and round, bore directly into him. Her high, wrinkled cheekbones framed a faint smile on her cracked lips which he noticed in the dimly lit living room. It seemed to Ron that her smile would coax the answer she needed from him. "Remember when I was pregnant and you came over and we talked about it?" she asked. Ron looked at her, stunned at how Linda's seemingly firm recollection collided with his own ignorance of a memory. "'Course you were drinkin' a lot then. It does things to your memory, maybe," she offered. Graciously she had given Ron the out he needed.

"Yeah, I guess all the booze really did fog my memory. Can't remember anything, really. Those days were really kind of bad for me, ya know."

"Yeah. Ever stay married to that Wendy gal?" Her question was perfunctory, knowing, as she did, more about the wreckage from his first marriage than Ron might remember she knew.

"All's I remember is the divorce," Ron said bitterly. He looked down between his knees. "Yeah, we had a kid and I spent most of the time fightin' her old man over the child support. Her old man's a lawyer, ya know. Turned out to be a real dipshit." Ron paused. Linda said nothing. "Yeah, but I settled down, though, and married a real nice little gal from Pendleton. Got two boys." Linda knew that the man wasn't about to admit to anyone that the real intensity of their relationship after the war — their coupling — happened when he drank — not only during his separation from Wendy, but before.

"Boys, huh?" Linda looked interested. "How old are they, Ron?"

"Well, my oldest boy by Wendy — Ed — he's in his twenties now. Melissa and I have two of our own. Robert, he's twelve and little Josh is about seven. A real handful." Linda smiled weakly over at him.

For a long half-minute, then, the Indian woman sat in her chair staring at the man she had known fifteen years earlier. They looked at each other with an awkward silence stretching between them. Finally, Linda Pawlik Whitman spoke. "What about your other boy, Ron? Sam."

"Sam." The name came out of Ron. Not a question, not a statement, just the name. "Well, Linda, I have to be kinda careful, ya know. Been advised not to make any of those..." Ron paused in mid sentence. "What do ya call them?" He glanced around the room as if expecting to find the answer written somewhere. "Admissions. That's what I was told. Not to make any of those admissions." An amused look overcame Linda's face. Ron chuckled, his earlier nervous guard beginning to drop away. Still, Ron felt he was being unwittingly snared into a trap, about to be sprung by a woman who thought he might be her youngster's father.

Looking at Linda's amused smile, he worried a little if she knew more than he did about the case. Ron Hathaway knew at that instant that he had a decision to make. Either go forward, or remain, forever, on the banks of the river.

"Is Sam here?" he asked Linda Whitman. Linda shifted slowly in her chair, looking down, displaying, now, a sadness in the corners of her mouth and in her eyes, as she painfully readjusted herself.

"No, Ron, Sam's not here." A long silence fell over the room. "He's run away." The thought sent Ron's head reeling, as if whitewater he had chosen to go through had suddenly become a boiling cauldron at the last second.

He felt that one horrifying moment on the Salmon River — when the oar snapped and Ed disappeared over the side into the abyss of "Demon's Drop." Ron shuddered inwardly, now, at the shock of Sam's disappearance.

"Do you know where he's gone?" Ron asked incredulously. "I've got to say, I'm a little bit surprised."

"I'm not," Sam's mother snapped back. The sharpness of her retort startled Ron. He did not want to push any further.

"Mom, are you coming to bed?" came Susan's voice. She held open her bedroom door, quietly explaining to her mother that it was now after 3:00 in the morning and that her mother needed her rest.

"Sure, honey, I'll be right in," she replied. "Is Sandy asleep?" she asked her daughter.

"Sure, Mom," replied Susan. Linda's daughter then glanced over at Ron. "Remember, Mom, Doris is coming tomorrow morning." A look on Susan's face told Ron it was time to leave.

"Be right in, honey." Linda seemed weary to Ron, more tired than he had ever seen her before. Again, he noticed the blotches and spots of hair missing from the side of Linda's head as she turned to address her daughter.

Ron tried to get up, his legs barely able to move. He looked over at Linda.

"Listen, Ron, I need to hit the sack but you're free to crash out here if you wanna," she offered. Ron smiled at her with a feeling of gratitude for allowing him to stay, instead of inviting him to leave which she could so easily have done.

"Thanks, Linda, I really appreciate that. It's been a long day, and I don't think my wife's gonna miss me much tonight."

Linda got up slowly from her old cushioned chair, bracing herself with both hands as she got up. She ambled slowly towards the bedroom door in the back next to the bedroom door where Susan had appeared.

"Conk yourself out, ol' man. Don't worry 'bout it," she said with the same casualness Ron remembered. "I've had a long, hard day too. See you in the mornin'," she gestured to him with her hand as she disappeared inside her bedroom and closed the door softly.

Ron settled back on the sunken sofa cushion, resting his head on both of the small, worn oval pillows. He felt a hard metal spring from beneath the sofa touch just under his right thigh.

The earlier sting of the hands from the cold night air had now subsided along with the brisk hot crispness of the coffee he had swallowed. The earlier effects of the booze swept back and forth now, his dark blood throbbing through his forehead and temples as he softly swayed towards unconsciousness.

CHAPTER 15

THE TAKEOUT POINT

Linda Whitman did not have an easy sleep that morning. Twice she arose from her bed, feeling her way through the dark living room, tripping once on the threadbare rug, and throwing herself in front of the toilet, vomiting until she was exhausted. Her last trip to the bathroom had left her sore knees resting on the cold linoleum floor, head thrown over the toilet, retching yellow bile. Drying herself off, she knew this was not from too much to drink, something she had faced often enough in the past.

Pale and exhausted, she finally sank down on her bed for the second time at the first light of dawn and fell into a restless, almost semiconscious doze, her face buried in her thin, lumpy pillow.

She opened her eyes, feeling something pressing at her side. Linda looked over and saw Susan standing by the bed, holding her month-old baby boy, Timothy, to her breast. Linda yawned and motioned for her daughter to sit.

"You O.K., Mom?" Susan asked, a sympathetic smile crossing her face as she cradled her baby. "Doris is fixin' us all breakfast."

"Oh, that's sweet," Linda whispered with a faint smile. "Honey, you go tell her that I'll be up in a minute." She paused, listening to the spitting sound of bacon and eggs frying on the gas stove in the small kitchen off in the back. Then she suddenly remembered. "Is Sam's dad still here?" she asked her daughter.

"Yeah, still asleep on the couch, I guess." Linda heard a growling intermixed with the cooking of the morning breakfast. Ron's long, alarm-like snores, mixed with throaty gurgling noises reawakened memories within Linda from long ago. "Jesus, the man sleeps like a foghorn," observed Susan. She and her mother laughed. "That was the first damn thing that woke me up this mornin', Mom. Had to pinch his nose a couple times. Still didn't work, though," added Susan with a disgusted look.

"Where's Sandy?" asked her mother.

"Out in the kitchen waitin' for breakfast," answered Susan, shifting Timothy to her opposite breast. Linda rolled onto her side, reaching under the sagging bed frame for something. Susan watched her mother's chunky hand move slowly under the bedspread. Finally the hand made contact, pulling out a metal-framed photograph. On it was the image of Samuel. Linda held it up to Susan.

"I threw this picture down here with his other stuff when he split. Made me so damn mad. Here, honey, you take this out and put it in the livin' room. When his dad wakes up, I want him to see his son," she instructed.

"Sure, Mom. Come on out and have some breakfast with us, will ya?"

"O.K., sweetie." Linda rested upright on her elbows. She smiled weakly at Susan. Cradling her baby and holding Sam's photograph in her left hand, Linda's daughter walked sideways through the bedroom door towards the front room couch.

Linda fell back in her bed, staring out the window where sunlight was filtering in from the brightly lit Saturday morning in early February.

It had been over a month since Sam had disappeared. She felt regret now, for the way she had told Sam the things that she thought he needed to know about her. The boy wasn't prepared. The strands of sunlight through the window touched the tears welling in Linda Pawlik's sunken eyes. Sam had gone into a world where he only half belonged. Her thoughts of him paralyzed her even more than her physical weakness. Her tears flowed easily, now, sliding down the deep crevices of her tired face.

Her father had never wanted to see his children cry. A tall, bandy-legged "rodeo wreck" with huge hands, he rode hard, smoked hard and drank hard. Pendleton roundup posters had always featured him gripping the thrashing bulls, his long black-braided hair flying in all directions. He worked as a janitor when he wasn't away from home rodeoing in towns like Haines or St. Paul or Prescott, Arizona, or at home mending his broken and bruised body.

Her father's family — related to the Nez Perce Whitman family line — were from a strong Presbyterian background. Joseph Whitman was his given Christian name. Like many present-day Native Americans, his family had turned to traditional religion. But not Joseph. He wanted people to call him Pawlik.

Falling into a semiconscious doze in her bed, images of Linda Pawlik's plump, soft-spoken mother, Bonnie, played across her mind. Linda had adored her mother. Her family, originally from the Umatilla Reservation, was a variety of Cayuse and Umatilla with an intermixing of Anglo blood from intermarriage with settlers in the region.

Linda smiled faintly. Little Pawlik's colored horse drawings reminded her of the talent Bonnie had given to her as a youngster — constantly sketching and painting the bulls and wild rodeo horses Joseph rode.

Linda and her mother saw less and less of Joseph Pawlik before Bonnie died giving birth to her fourth child.

Linda hated her stepmother, Marielle. This slender, beautifully chiseled Hispanic woman seemed to take more of her father's attention. They partied and Linda learned to raise her five younger siblings. Bonnie had been a good teacher.

After Joseph Pawlik died from cancer, Linda had forgotten her father's jealousy and drunken episodes with Marielle. She saw the bruises on pretty Marielle's face and arms now and heard the thump of her stepmother being slammed against the kitchen wall of their old tar-papered shack.

The explosion at the end of the shotgun startled her awake as Salvador's unturned face appeared, his voice quivering her name. Her small bedroom twisted upside down as Linda felt her head hit the dash when her car smashed into the concrete that night. She saw, for the last time, little Roberto's cherubic face, those beautiful dark brown eyes and his little smile, always forming that high arch from his upper lip.

Linda sobbed, a deep heave rolling in waves from within her belly to her shoulders, bringing forth her worst nightmare, hidden from Susan and Little Pawlik all these years.

Her first born, Patricia Whitecloud, had been removed because of the vileness of the man she had killed. The guilt was not so much because of the infant — the baby boy Sal had fathered by Patricia was adopted out to a Nez Perce couple in Lapwai, Idaho. It was because she had not given her daughter the safety that Bonnie taught her a mother always gives her children. Patricia ran away from her foster parents to a street life of powder, needles and prostitution. The news of her murder in Seattle — they had found her body in a dank hotel room, brutalized repeatedly with a knife — had reached her through Doris Wallport.

Linda Pawlik Whitman lay there for a long time, the dirty shadowed ceiling closing down on her as if it were the lid to her coffin.

Finally, the smell of bacon from the kitchen awoke her. Her friend Doris, her mainstay and, to Linda, the only other adult in this world, was fixing breakfast this Saturday morning, as she always had for the past several months.

Linda's eyebrows narrowed as she smelled her stale pillow. What had Ron Hathaway become? She furrowed her brow deeper. The fact that Linda knew Ron was Sam's father made her resent him even more. He was a total stranger to the boy. And to her. And to her family. She felt the bitterness start to tear at her insides, making foul the taste of her swallow.

Moving her head slowly, she squinted at the incoming bands of sunlight from the window, intruding like metal-tipped claws reminding her that Ron's sudden presence was forced upon them now by the state's paternity case. Even if Sam came back, would he want to see his father?

Forgetting the dryness in her throat, the dizzying nausea and the weakness, her thoughts returned to those few people who were with her now — Doris, Susan, and the children. She could hear their hushed talking in the kitchen, as if they were awaiting the arrival of the family's matriarch.

The Indian woman slowly lifted herself off the bed, upright onto the floor. As she tied the thick drawstring to her bathrobe and tightened the knot across her protruding stomach with a firm tug, Linda Whitman made a decision this cold, sunny Saturday morning.

She strode through her bedroom door, glancing into the living room, seeing where Susan had placed Samuel's picture, conspicuously poised on the small table in front of the couch, probably the first thing Ron would see when he awoke. Turning to her right, she walked slowly out into the kitchen, rubbing the sleep from her eyes, greeting everyone with a quiet hello and, finally, giving Doris a big hug.

"How you feeling, luv?" asked Doris, a broad grin on her face. "Susan here's been telling me about a gentleman caller last night," she joked. "One thing hasn't changed in the man over fifteen years." She paused. "Still snores like a cannon." They all laughed.

"Sandy," Linda wryly admonished her youngest son, "go in there and pinch what's-his-name's nose, so he stops snoring, O.K.?" The pint-sized, dark-haired youngster seated at the table jumped up with a gleeful smile and raced into the living room. Presently, the snoring rattled rather abruptly. Then, with a few spasmodic gurgles and gulps, the snoring sputtered to a final stop, as the man, still unconscious, his Caterpillar hat lying on the floor, turned onto his side and farted, his back facing Samuel's picture. The boy ran back into the kitchen, smiling triumphantly at Doris and Linda, gleeful that he had just successfully completed the sneak attack on the stranger in the living room.

"What are you gonna talk to him about when he wakes up, hon?" asked Doris. She poured Linda a cup of hot coffee, and handed it to her as Linda seated herself at the kitchen table closest to where Doris was working by the stove. "Not gonna tell him about the paternity case, I hope," came Doris' answer to her own question. Doris had a worried look.

"No way in hell," replied Linda. Linda took several sips of hot coffee from her golden mug. That last phone conversation she'd had with the investigator — that Mr. Jacobs — from the state of Oregon had been like the hammer of truth coming down on the top of her head. Linda felt her forehead throb. As she took another sip from her mug, a faint smile overtook her — how silly, she thought, recalling a few hours back when Ron had mentioned not wanting to make any "admissions."

The sounds of groaning in the living room awoke Linda from her thoughts. Every sound in the small apartment except the frying bacon on the kitchen stove came to a halt. Linda and her family listened intently to the sounds of the man as he awoke. Linda glanced out at the couch. The corners of her mouth edged into a grin. From experience, she knew that Ron's awakening would prompt the dreaded pounding and hammering of a hangover at his forehead and his temples. Gingerly swinging his legs around in front of him, Ron bowed his hatless head, both hands slowly massaging his forehead and temples.

"Ohhh, man! What a hell of a way to get up in the mornin'," he wailed, his eyes still closed as he continued rubbing his pounding temples with both his thumbs.

"You should try gettin' up inside my head every mornin'," said Linda, grinning over at him. Ron Hathaway glanced up, a slight smile on his pale face.

"'Mornin', Linda. Thanks for lettin' me spend the night." Then the man closed his eyes again and returned to slowly fingering his temples. Doris, plate of bacon and eggs and toast in hand, poked her head around the corner and entered the living room, placing the plate on the table in front of Ron, next to the picture. Ron, catching the plate, glanced up.

"Ron, you remember Babs?" Linda said as she motioned towards her friend who was now serving him breakfast.

"Yeah," replied Ron. "Howdy."

"Hi Ron, good to see ya again. It's Doris Wallport. You remember?" she formally introduced herself, as she turned again towards the kitchen. Seeing Doris' stout frame and the broad expanse of her hips brought an immediate thought of Babs, the standoffish one. Ron had talked to Babs about the pregnancy.

"God, Doris it's been a long time. Sure nice to see ya. Wow. What a surprise." The suddenness of Doris' appearance distracted Ron from the pain at his forehead and temples. Doris quickly disappeared into the kitchen, reappearing again with a cup of coffee which she gingerly placed next to the picture.

Glancing over at the steaming cup, Ron Hathaway saw the metal-framed photograph. Hot, pounding waves slowly returned to his forehead. Linda watched Ron from the kitchen, setting her coffee mug on the counter. Slowly, she walked towards her old stuffed chair.

"That's a nice picture of Sam," remarked Ron calmly while slowly massaging his temples. "He's a good lookin' boy, Linda. I seen a picture of him when the blood test results came back, a real nice lookin' kid." Ron slowly nodded his head up and down while the massaging continued, as if approving of the boy's physical attributes. Linda, staring at him, laughed to herself, offended at the triteness of Ron's compliment.

"Well, why don't you eat your breakfast first, ol' man and then we can talk, O.K.?" The suggestion seemed to reassure Ron.

As he slowly ate, the conversation turned to Sandy and Susan's baby. Ron and Doris talked about old times. He complimented her on her change of life, being able to move from Pendleton to Eugene. After all, he explained to her, he had done the same thing after his divorce.

Linda, too, began to sense this rapport they all had. Strangers, really, to each other now, but folks who had grown up together a long time ago in Pendleton and had come through a geographic odyssey separately, but converging, finally, in this tiny apartment fifteen years later in the town of Eugene.

After Ron's second helping of bacon and eggs, his third cup of coffee and a trip to the bathroom, he settled back. Finally putting on his Caterpillar hat, Linda was amused once again at his distinctive protruding ears.

"Hey, ol' man, you still got them cute little Martian ears I liked so much," she chided. "Just like Sam does," she chuckled again, noticing the sudden change in Ron's expression.

Then just as suddenly, she saw him hesitate and grin knowingly at her. "Yeah, used to attract all the women," he laughed in a relaxed sort of way that made Linda feel that he was actually poking fun at himself. Self-effacing almost. How much better, she thought, if Sam could have had this man to teach him confidence.

Linda continued examining the man intently, noticing the grime and oil that had worked its way into his fingers and hands, crusty and weatherworn from working as a carpenter. Under his half-opened blue and white flannel shirt, she could tell that the man still had that lean, well-muscled body so familiar to her fifteen years ago.

Ron Hathaway continued rubbing his temples, sipping his coffee. Resting the cup softly on the table, his eyes focused on Sam's picture.

He had rambled on, that one night at her place, about his days in the infantry — as a "leg" in the war. The loss of his buddy Leo. The sex they had had that same night seemed to her not so much a sharing as his desperate attempt to grasp a pleasure, an elusive something that to Ron might mean the be-all and end-all of his very existence.

No, he wouldn't have remembered that night. It wasn't unusual for him to black out. He had blacked out that night, too, not remembering the sweat his body had generated during the effort, lying exhausted and unconscious afterwards. She wondered if she should tell him.

"Did you ever go see Leo's folks?" Linda broke in. "You told me you were goin'. Remember?"

Ron stared at Linda for a long moment. "Yeah. Finally decided to see Leo's folks in LA," he started out slowly. A look of recognition slowly crept across his face. Linda nodded.

"How'd it go?"

"Was tough. But I felt good about going." Ron took a sip of coffee and looked down at his feet. "Found out his dad was disabled — a bad fall at work. Drank a lot while I was there." Ron spoke haltingly, as if wanting to forget. "Lots of family. Mother's real nice. Cleans houses." He broke off, still staring at the floor.

"Ever show them those pictures of Leo?" she asked. That night Ron had shown Linda the pictures of his buddy standing next to a latrine in a floppy bush hat and jungle fatigues.

"Sure did." Ron looked up at Linda again. "Gave 'em copies. No way I was gonna part with the originals." He grinned. Linda could see his hands trembling.

"Ron, remember talkin' to me about comin' to the hospital when I had Sam?" interjected Linda. Ron glanced over at her with a puzzled look, his mouth slightly open. "You know, I asked you to come over to the hospital? Remember?" Ron seemed perplexed at the suddenness of it all.

"Yeah, I guess I never did get around to comin' out to the hospital," he slowly replied. Ron paused a long moment and then looked up at Linda. "You know I left Pendleton right after I last saw you...."

Linda glanced over at her friend Doris, standing at the opening to the kitchen, looking at Ron, now, and listening intently. Little or no emotion was displayed on either of the women's faces. The long silence was finally broken by Linda's daughter.

"Well, your youngest boy — what did you say his name was?"

"Josh," replied Ron.

"Yes, Josh. He must be just like little Sandy here," explained Susan, pointing to the boy who was squirming under the kitchen table with his toy cars.

Ron laughed and took another sip of his coffee, deliberately taking off his Caterpillar hat and setting it on the table next to Sam's picture.

"Linda, can you tell me what you told Sam about me?" The Indian woman stared at the man, who was only now signaling more than casual approval at the youngster's physical appearance.

"Well, Doris here helped to raise Sam," replied Linda.

"She helped raise me and Sam," broke in Susan. "Used to tell us wonderful stories about our heritage and all. You know we're Nez Perce?" Ron nodded and smiled knowingly.

"Well, actually I helped Linda out, here, when she had troubles of her own and we all did the best we could," volunteered Doris Wallport. Doris now walked between Linda and Ron and sat down at the opposite end of the couch from Ron, calmly smoothing back her brown, uncombed hair which touched just above the collar of the red sweater she wore around her sturdy frame. At five-foot-five, she was just about Linda's height, but carried slightly less weight, her wide hips and legs contoured beneath loosely fitting white slacks, the ends of which ended above slightly pudgy feet tucked into worn brown flats. She crossed one leg over the other now as she sat opposite Ron on the couch. Shifting slightly towards Ron, she placed her outstretched right hand atop the worn couch almost as a gesture of goodwill to him.

"Babs here is part family to us," chimed in Linda. Doris smiled at her friend.

"Yeah, we told him about you, Ron," said Doris with a deliberate nod of her head. "Right after he visited Hathaway Hardware Store, he became interested in boats." Squinting his eyes, Ron looked stunned. "Used to love to draw horses, too," remarked Doris. "Would light up when I'd tell him those stories about the Nez Perce and their horses," she chuckled, glancing over now at Linda. Both women laughed.

"He's pretty good at fixin' things, too," remarked Sam's mother. "Has kept my car up and runnin' way past its time," she said with pride.

Ron's stunned look now was transformed to one of intense interest. "How's he doin' in school?" he asked.

"Doesn't do well at all," replied his mother bluntly. "Reacts too damn fast with his fists," she added. "Can't control the boy no more," she went on, a frown crossing Linda's face. "Yeah, the times that Sam liked to draw horses reminds me of when he had a name for you, ol' man," she said. "Used to call you 'Great Horse.'"

A slow smile crept across Ron Hathaway's face, now, as he looked directly at Linda. "Really?" he said. "Why would he call me that?" He looked amazed and perplexed all at once.

"Because you were his hero," explained Doris Wallport. "After we took him to Old Joseph's grave, and he saw your yearbook picture, you became his greatest Nez Perce warrior."

For once, Linda was truly grateful for the Indian stories and myths that her friend had taught her two children. She noticed Ron's adam's apple move up and down beneath his red weather-beaten neck as he swallowed hard. Seeing the man now struggling, she decided it was finally time to confront him.

"Why won't you acknowledge your own boy?" The intensity and piercing of her voice startled even Doris. Ron half rose, as if to go. "God damn it, Ron!"

"Calm down now, luv," Doris beckoned.

Linda held her head high, her breath bursting forth through flared nostrils. Her dark-set eyes, at first narrowed, were now wide, aiming at the top of Ron's head.

"No I won't, damn it!" she shot back, holding up her trembling hand to Ron. "Sit down, ol' man," she commanded.

In that instant, Linda's eyes — dark, angry, sunken wells — consumed Ron and became for him the terrifying vent holes he so narrowly missed falling into above "The Queen" mine, where once he had feared little Melissa had been lost. The jarring thought cut through him — a silent electric shock — forcing him to sit down.

Sandy was at the front door now, Susan following close, holding her baby. The door slammed shut. Doris quietly got up and walked to the kitchen. No one said a word.

"What's there to say?" Ron finally managed with a pleading look, both arms outstretched. "You know I can't talk about the trial," he said almost in a whisper. Linda looked over at Ron Hathaway, slouched on her couch, his face embarrassingly diverted from hers. Her dark eyes, set back in her drawn face, were unblinking for a long time.

"Why are you deny'n paternity?" she asked, slowly shaking her head. "Damn it, man. You know you're Sam's father!" Ron Hathaway shrugged, offering her only a guilty look.

"Ya gotta believe me, Linda, you know it's the way the damn state works," he replied. "Hell, I didn't get the letter from the state until fifteen years late," he continued. "What do you expect me to do. You know I've got a family and three kids. What the hell am I supposed ta do with the state jumpin' all over my butt asking for $26,000?" Linda continued to stare, unmoved.

"Well, yeah, that is a lot of money, ol' man. But, ya know, I don't really have any control over that," she added. "Bein' on welfare, I do as I'm told." She looked at him hard. "You know money's not my worry ol' man," she continued. "I'm more concerned about my boy." She paused. "Our boy." Linda's single-minded look bore right into Ron Hathaway's forehead, still warm from the effects of the booze he had consumed the night before.

"Well, do you know where Sam's run off to?" asked Ron.

"Well, we think with some street kids, maybe a fellow named Strickler," replied Doris from the kitchen. "That's what we're afraid of, ya know. The Strickler kid is really an outlaw. Into drugs and stuff. Not good for Sam at all," she said.

The two women were immediately struck by the nervous rubbing of Ron Hathaway's hands together, over and over and over, followed by his slowly picking up the metal-framed photograph of Samuel Little Pawlik Whitman.

* * * * *

Ron Hathaway looked at the boy whose image was displayed in the inexpensive colored photograph which he held in his hands before him in the living room of the little apartment occupied by those in the young man's life who were closest and dearest to him.

The soft light from the window behind him played on the glass of the framed picture, casting a glimmer of his own reflection. It melted together all at once with the image of the boy.

Ron saw himself in the image. It flooded back in on him now — the connection, the choice he made so long ago below "Demon's Drop." He had made the decision to commit — to teach his children. He saw in the boy's crop of black hair his own dad's crop of coal black hair stuffed beneath his cap those summers they fished and the folks at the Troy Café laughed at his father's outlandish stories. The boy's protruding ears brought back his little hoot owl waving high above the John Day. The dark, lively eyes and slightly crooked grin betrayed that unpredictable quality. He wondered how the boy might handle a chance encounter with a western rattler.

Staring at the boy's image, the chords of Ron Hathaway's past at once became the architecture of his vision of Sam.

Finally, he nodded over to Doris, thanking her for breakfast and the coffee. His eyes met Linda Whitman's, the Indian girl he had confided in so long ago, telling her things about the life within him which had all but disappeared from his memory after fifteen long years.

Amidst the thrashing waves of booze, perhaps their time together might have produced something, he thought. Yet there remained things that Ron Hathaway could not yet fully understand. The court case was a barrier of fear. A gulf of doubt and denial lay within him like the immovable river boulders he had learned to avoid during his white-water journeys.

He held out both of his hands to Linda, not waiting for her to rise from her chair, telling her that he must go now. He had to see his wife, Melissa. Linda, hoping to reassure Ron, explained to him that she was sure that Melissa would understand — that under the circumstances this had been an important meeting for all of them.

Clasping Linda's right hand with both of his, Ron Hathaway sensed something deep within her, something too deep for her to share with him now. With arms trembling, Linda gingerly lifted herself up from her chair. It was her inner strength which dictated to this woman that their parting must be dignified, with her fully on her feet. It meant much more than a simple social amenity.

"I'll be in touch," Ron stated, looking directly at her. Linda nodded.

As he drove back across town in his rig, Ron Hathaway thought of just what he would do and say at the trial. Still, what could he possibly say after having met Linda and having experienced the past few hours?

What would he tell Melissa when he got home? He decided he would tell her that he had gone over to Linda's. But how would he explain to Melissa why he had lost his job?

Ron's head started pounding again.

What about Sam? Then a thought suddenly struck him. Sam had vanished.

CHAPTER 16

THE JOY OF FATHERHOOD

I reached over to the stack of mail piled high on my desk that cold, snowy Monday afternoon in late February and tore open the envelope from the state of Oregon.

Inside, a letter accompanied a copy of a motion for a dismissal order which the state had recently filed in Ron Hathaway's paternity case. I read the letter:

"After due consideration, the state hereby elects to dismiss the within captioned paternity action because of the length of time which has elapsed as well as considerations of the mother's health."

The letter wasn't even signed by Felicia Simmons. The state says "never mind," just like that. I stared at the letter, repeating the thought again. I shook my head at the concise formality, suggesting no recognition of what really had happened. A "good" result for my people. I felt a cold twinge of cynicism.

I picked up the phone and dialed, expecting Melissa to answer, as she had so often before. I was anxious to tell her the good news. Instead, I heard Ron Hathaway's low, subdued voice over the phone.

"Ron, I've got some good news for you. How come you're not at work?"

"I lost my job at Dahlberg," came the faraway, groping reply. "Melissa's staying with the kids at her folks in Pendleton," he explained.

"Ron, how is your diversion program going?" I asked, hoping to hear some good news.

"Going just fine," he replied somewhat dryly. "The counseling is so damned expensive. Been goin' to AA meetings twice a week — every Tuesday and Thursday," he added.

"Part of the diversion program?"

"Not really." He paused, "An old river drifting buddy from Pendleton said it might be worthwhile."

"And?"

"Meetings are full of caffeine addicts. Everyone drinks gallons of coffee." We both laughed. "A lot of Nam vets go, though. It's kind'a nice to talk to guys who've been through it."

"How's Melissa?" I asked.

"Guess my drinkin' has messed things up." Ron paused. "Don't really blame her, though. She deserves better."

"You're a lucky man, Ron," I offered. "Don't blow it."

"I won't," he said with an unfamiliar firmness. "I remember how lucky I felt, especially when we met in Eugene, before we got married." Ron's spirits seemed altogether buoyed by the thought. "By the way, what's the good news?" he asked anxiously.

"Well, Ron, the state has decided to dismiss the paternity case because of our legal arguments." I raised myself up in my chair as if to try and lift Ron's spirits. But inside I was feeling no real joy.

"That's fantastic!" Ron said enthusiastically. "Melissa will really be glad to hear that," he added, a bounce coming back to his voice. "But I don't know. I guess things just haven't worked out. I'm trying, though. Been lookin' for new work with another construction outfit here in Springfield. They might have some work in Medford. By the way, does this mean that Linda and Sam are out of the picture?"

Ron's question, almost an afterthought, meant that I had to unravel for him the whole, sad story.

"No," I replied. "It only means that the state has dismissed this particular paternity action. It was filed on behalf of the state agency which paid the public assistance to Linda and Sam over the years," I explained. "You may still be faced with a paternity action from Linda herself or from the boy. Especially from Sam. They could decide, later on, that you are the father. They could, conceivably, pursue the matter on their own." There was a long pause from both of us on either end of the phone. I waited for a response, hoping Ron might change the subject.

"What do you think the chances are of them doing that?" His voice sounded anxious again. "I just can't go through this mess anymore." His voice was shaking. He fell silent for a second. "For God's sake," he implored. "Do you really think I'll get sued over this again?"

"I don't really know," I went on. "It seems unlikely, Ron. Sam is a runaway — has outstanding warrants for drug possession and car theft." I paused one more agonizing moment. "Linda may be terminally ill," I finally told him. Jessie had reluctantly given me some of the sketchy details.

"Jesus," I heard Ron say.

I explained that Linda Whitman had tried her best to survive but in the end she was battling either ovarian cancer or cancer of the cervix, I wasn't sure. She had had a hysterectomy. This was followed by devastating radiation and chemotherapy treatments in Portland and Eugene. Jessie had told me that while her cancer had been in remission, she looked forward to attending the trial. Now the cancer had come back and was not going away. It had spread. She would not be able to testify. The only trial this poor woman was going through was her own.

I was tired. As I explained all of these things to Ron, the words of Supreme Court Justice John Paul Stevens came back to me. "The actions of judges neither create nor sever genetic bonds."

I wondered. After fifteen years, it did not seem likely to me that this man would ever contribute to young Samuel Whitman's life. Paternity case or no paternity case. Perhaps the distance of time had severed Ron from Sam. Perhaps it was much more.

"You know, Ron," I continued. "You might want to give Linda a call and discuss the situation with her privately." The suggestion came out of me more as an expression of what I considered to be the "moral" thing to do rather than as a means for Ron to simply reassure himself. I waited. There was an unusually long pause at the other end of the phone.

"Do they know where Sam has run off to?" he quietly asked me. I detected almost a humility to his voice. Why had he asked me this question? I wondered.

"No, I don't know where he's run off to," I replied. I sensed that Ron felt safe — now that the pressure was off. We had just won a victory at the hands of the state of Oregon. "Maybe you should call Linda. Really," I added. "There's no longer a legal situation. Maybe she'll want to talk to you and so will Sam," I suggested. "Think about it, will you?"

"O.K., I'll think it over," he replied.

"Can I call you, then, if I find anything out, or if Sam returns?" I knew that my feelings might be misconstrued, that my suggestion might be rebuffed by a man who really, down deep, felt that he had nothing in common with a youngster he had sired but had not seen in fifteen years.

"I'd like that, counselor," said Ron softly. "I want him to meet Great Horse."

Hearing this strange remark made me think he'd been drinking again. Yet he wanted to see the boy.

I bid Ron Hathaway good luck and put the phone down gently. I leaned back, placed my hands behind my head and glanced outside, noticing how the leafless birch and maple trees with pointed branches were sparring with each other in the snow-driven wind. Flakes softly touched the window and were transformed silently into tiny droplets from the building's inner heat — a stark contrast to the pelt of rain-drops which so often accompanied the frequent Willamette Valley storms. Everything outside seemed quiet, all sounds muted by the crystal white blanket which draped everything. Way off in the distance, a low fog shroud hid the tops of the downtown skyscrapers.

Nearer, across the bridge, I watched the flag waving freely atop the girdled dome of the State Office Building. I imagined the people inside that tall, domed State Office Building. I imagined how they must all be going through their daily routines, sending out their letters.

I paused in mid thought. How much more difficult was it for men in Ron Hathaway's situation to grasp the opportunities of fatherhood? Does the fact that a woman gives birth to a child from her womb make parent-hood inherently more difficult for the male of the species to grasp?

I thought of two fathers. Chief Joseph had been a father to his people at a dark time in the history of the Nez Perce. Another man had been called "father Abraham" by the slaves at a time when he attempted to appeal to the higher instincts of a nation torn asunder at the beginning of a tragic civil war.

Thinking of these two men, I sat staring at the dark gray wall-fountain framed by the dome of the State Office Building, its pond a white frozen sheen, its once cascading fountain now a dry, stoney wall empty of water and people.

I settled back in my chair. A profound tiredness lifted me slowly as I drifted off.

Then it came to me as though it had been there for a hundred thousand years but only recently blunted by a culture which pandered to a kind of consuming adult hedonism. It was bathed in a cleansing fresh-ness, with the odor of a very ancient primal instinct, as sure as the crest-ing and falling of the waves from nature's tides. Almost imperceptively, the fountain pool and wall, with its cantilevered trough, melted and soft-ened, blurred by the sleepy, snowy mist from the drifting. Then it trans-formed to new shadows. I peered into the velvety serene vision, hoping to catch a glimpse, some clue, of the Indian boy.

Off to the side, on the pebbled embankment beneath the shadows of the over-arching firs, a woman was seated, watching a young boy tossing small stones into the deep pond. The indentations rippled out, disappearing beneath the water cascade from the slide. At the base of the rock wall stood a young man, hands extended on a frayed rope ladder, looking up at a little boy, seated at the top of the concave in the rock, wildly and triumphantly waving to the woman below. Glancing upward, the woman waved back.

Crawling across the rock outcropping at the top, the Indian boy's coal black hair was askew, the sunlight finding his shiny silver ring in the left ear and casting a diamond glint at the edge of the dream. Behind the beaming, waving child was saddled a dark-haired man, bolt upright, warrior-like, in the rock concave — as if astride a giant stone stallion, its neck lowered, drinking from the pond.

The Indian boy crawled towards the dark-haired warrior who turned and looked at the boy. The boy stopped — transfixed — as if frozen by fear. Then slowly the warrior beckoned to the Indian boy with both arms outstretched and the father embraced his son there at the top.

Startled by an impulse I did not fully understand, I awoke and picked up the telephone, dialing the number for Doreen Wilshire, my friend at the Support Enforcement Division's office in Portland.

"Hi, Doreen. Is Jessie in the office today? Can you patch me through to him, please?" I asked rather tentatively. At first not even sure what I was going to discuss with Jessie on such a blind impulse, I hesitated.

"Well, hello again, stranger," Doreen said, immediately recognizing my voice. I always marveled at Doreen's uncanny ability to place a voice with a person's identity, despite the hundreds of calls she fielded each day. "Sure, the big man's in town today. Just give me a second and I'll patch you right back to him."

"Hello, counselor," came Jessie's deep, reassuring voice. I chuckled as I heard his chair squeak and groan beneath his immense weight. Hearing the big man's baritone again, this devoted foster parent and proud "coach" of three beautiful daughters and two grand-daughters, struck the chord. I decided why I had made the call to Jessie this cold, snowy Monday afternoon. It was, after all, part of the work I had committed myself to perform. Fatherhood, like parenthood itself, is not a visceral instinct born from our sexual desire as mammals to procreate. It is a work which finds its genesis in the human heart — the Spirit Force Joseph had known — and springs forth as the innate desire we all have to covet, in the words of father Abraham, "the better angels of our nature."

"Hey, Jessie. Remember the Hathaway case?"

"Sure," he replied.

"Jessie, do you think we can find the boy, Sam?" I asked.

EPILOGUE

The boy entered the small bedroom. She had been in and out of delirium for about a week. He stared across the room at his mother's sunken face, her body covered with the pink and red-quilted bed sheet.

The boy walked slowly towards the foot of the bed, noticing, again, his mother's eyes fixed on him. Her head, slightly propped by a dirty white chiffon pillow, rested next to the circular bedstand where a box of Kleenex and a half-empty glass of water sat, the straw protruding at a crooked angle. The small bedroom was cluttered with clothes, boxes, medicines. The boy's metal-framed picture was propped next to the bedstand.

"She's awake now," said the heavyset woman standing in the doorway.

The boy turned toward the woman, "Does she still recognize me?"

"Sure," she replied as the woman walked to the foot of the bed.

His mother wanted to finish so many small tasks. Her friend had told her not to worry — she'd take care of things.

Turning, the boy reached out and touched his mother's face, her head now almost totally without hair, stray clumps here and there mixed with short stark strands of dark hair lying atop a blotched skin landscape, a strange bony appearance. He bent down and kissed the side of his mother's cheek, then the top of her head. Her trembling, swollen hand came out and met his and he sat on the edge of the bed.

"Mom?" Sunlight coming through the window cast a glint off the boy's earring which caught his mother's eye.

"Hey there," she paused, the boy listening to her labored breathing coming in irregular patterns. The Indian woman glanced over at her friend, motioning to her with her glistening eyes. Her friend approached as the boy's mother struggled to sit upright. Protruding from beneath the bed sheets, the boy beheld his mother's feet, swollen and almost purplish, her toenails jagged and broken.

"Mom, have you finished your painting?" Her vision would usually come when she was exhausted and the boy always listened.

His mother's head now leaned into his shoulder and she slowly nodded. The boy knew what she meant.

"Yes," she barely whispered. "My horse is completed."

"Mom, is the horse near the waterfall yet?"

"Yes, son, it is drinking from the pond now."

"What about Great Horse, Mom?"

Her breathing came in shallow, labored sighs, now. "Yes, he's on the horse." A long moment passed. "I can get on the horse now — he's gonna take me away." He was holding her just then. It was like the time at the hospital in the stark white room, alone with his mother. He was a brave — a survivor.

The boy glanced over at the woman who nodded, for he knew that this was what his mother had wanted, and he had wanted this for her, too.

Hearing his mother's breathing stop, the boy laid his mother back down on the bed, glancing one more time at her beautiful dark eyes. Reaching out, he touched her forehead with his finger and then he closed her eyelids for the final time.

The boy got up slowly and stepped backwards towards the bedroom door as the large woman came around from behind. Turning, he felt her large, soft head pressed next to his as they hugged.

Then the boy strode towards the front door, opened it and looked out into the hot July air at the old Ford pickup parked on the street with the drift boat on top. And the boy remembered, again, what his father had told him — that the Rogue was an especially dangerous and beautiful rock garden this time of year.

The End